THE GIFT OF
DREAD

*How Your Search for Meaning
in Life can Lead to God*

ALBERT D. SPALDING, JR.

Gospel Apologetics
1700 Prestwick Road
313-218-3625
Gospel Apologetics, LLC

ISBN: 978-0-578-21546-4 (sc)
ISBN: 978-0-578-21547-1 (e)

Lulu Publishing Services rev. date: 02/08/2019

PREFACE

Twenty-first century post-modernism has become both a favorite whipping-boy and something of a conundrum for many of today's evangelists and social commentators. Many evangelical Christian churches and pastors in North America, for example, have spoken out against such features of post-modernism as its critique of language, its cynicism toward meta-narratives, and its representation of a cultural drift away from critical thinking. To some extent, these efforts seem to criticize current Western culture without necessarily engaging it effectively for the Gospel. The project of finding ways to articulate the Gospel in a manner that resonates with, and impacts, a post-modern culture is still a work in progress. This book seeks to participate in this project by considering the possibility that a poignant and profound discourse about the Gospel of Jesus Christ can reasonably emerge from a shared exploration of, and appreciation for, existential dread.

Existential dread, as it will be defined and considered in this work, refers to the sense of anxiety and restlessness that can be experienced by individuals who are (unsuccessfully) seeking to understand, clarify, and find ultimate meaning and coherence in their lives. It is proposed here that when such dread serves to propel individuals along a journey toward finding purposefulness and meaning, it is a gift. As part of this inquiry into the potential benefit of dread-driven meaning-seeking, the philosophical, psychological, and theological aspects of existential dread are taken into account.

The central concern, then, of this project is the problem of evangelism within a post-modern Western culture. How can the Gospel be properly and effectively introduced to nonbelievers who view its texts and truth-claims with suspicion, skepticism and cynicism? What common ground can the evangelist find with the post-modernist? How can the Gospel be more effectively introduced to individuals and groups who are influenced by a Western post-modern culture?

The possibility being explored here is the development of those questions and considerations that the evangelist or apologist might use in order to set the stage for the Gospel by first focusing on existential *angst*. The assumption here is that such dread seems to be at least as intense or prevalent within a 21st century post-modern Western culture as it has been at any other time or place. This book explores the apparent connection between "existential dread," and "meaning-seeking," and inquires into the apologetic implications of that apparent connection. It suggests that meaning-seeking is both a common human tendency and a virtue that can, and probably should, be artfully promoted by evangelists. The quest for meaning in life, as it has been studied and engaged within both the psychological and philosophical disciplines, is considered. Søren Kierkegaard's articulation of existential dread, and the implications of his work for post-modern cultures, is given special attention. Dread, it is concluded, can be a gift when it leads to meaning-seeking, which in turn can lead to a sober and honest consideration of the claims of the Gospel.

ACKNOWLEDGMENTS

Words cannot express my gratitude for the support, encouragement, prayers and most of all, patience, of my wife, Nancy, throughout the many years during which this project was being developed. Our son, Richard, and his wife Ju Hyung, as well as our daughter, Abigail, and her husband, Brian, have also provided encouragement in many different ways (including the occasional needling questions as to whether I would ever actually finish...). Thank you.

What I have found particularly touching and humbling have been the faithful inquiries from brothers and sisters in the Lord, including my pastors (senior pastor Bob Johnson and associate pastor David Dunham) and my brothers and sisters in the Lord at Cornerstone Baptist Church, Roseville, Michigan. Our small group and our Koinonia adult Bible fellowship, as well as many of the staff members and other good friends at church, have been a particularly generous and consistent source of encouragement. My personal prayer partners, Jeff Mantei, Dennis Ginnart, Keith Kaynor, Tony Griffin, Dave Sarakun, Larry Hait, Ron Cieslak, Wayne Wegner and the late Bob Clarke have had an immeasurable impact on me and on this work. Each of you kindly and generously asked me on a regular basis about the progress of this project, and you faithfully offered to pray for me as I have worked on it. Thank you, each one of you, and I apologize for not naming every one of you but there are page limits for these acknowledgments!

I am also indebted to Dr. Edward N. Martin, who generously held over and continued to serve on my dissertation committee – in order to see me through this project – even though his responsibilities elsewhere caused him to terminate his formal affiliation with Trinity Theological Seminary. And to Dr. David P. Meyer, who agreed to take over as the chair of my committee upon Dr. Martin's departure from Trinity. Thank you both for seeing me through to the completion of this project, and thank you for the many insights you have brought to me. (I am confident that the notion of "spectrum of authenticity" will be developed further in the future!)

I am also indebted to the group of Christian faculty, staff, student organization leaders and Central Alliance Church members who have been so encouraging and so faithful in prayer (and good advice) during our Monday prayer meetings near the Wayne State University campus.

Finally, last but not least, I am thankful for three most excellent proofreaders and editors: my sister-in-law and professional translator and wordsmith, Sharon Winkler Moren (who provided excellent suggestions for content as well as for the removal of extra commas and such); my friend and professional colleague, Dinah Tolbert; and my dear departed sister (and occasional co-author), the late Professor Rita A. Franks who served as Executive Director of Libraries at Louisiana Tech University.

To my wife, Nancy, with gratitude and love

CONTENTS

1

INTRODUCTION

Tell all the Truth but tell it slant —
Success in Circuit lies
Too bright for our infirm Delight
The Truth's superb surprise

As Lightning to the Children eased
With explanation kind
The Truth must dazzle gradually
Or every man be blind —

Emily Dickinson[1]

---

[1] Emily Dickinson, *The Complete Poems of Emily Dickinson*, No. 1129 (Boston: Little, Brown, 1960), pp. 506-507.

A Conversion Rejected

James sat quietly and politely in the third row of the little red brick church in Ypsilanti, Michigan on that hot summer morning in 1973. He was a 23-year-old college student, working part-time as a salesperson at a musical instruments and equipment store. He tried to be invisible. He tried not to stick to the varnished pew. He tried not to offend (even though his ponytail may have been offense enough for some of the closely cropped folks there). He was in attendance on that Sunday morning for only one reason: to complete the sale of a set of amplifiers, microphones, speakers and other sound equipment. He was not there to get "saved."

Within about five minutes into the sermon, though, he knew that he had been "had." He had been invited by the pastor into that church that morning, not only to help the church finalize its decision to purchase the sound equipment, but also, apparently, to allow him to hear the Gospel. The pastor was using James' desire to close a sale as a means to get him into the church, so that he might accept Jesus Christ as his personal Lord and Savior.

Back in the showroom of the music store earlier that week, James had enjoyed his initial conversations with the pastor. After demonstrating a sound system for about an hour, James was assured by the pastor that the church was likely to purchase the system. However, the pastor asked James to bring the equipment to the church, set it up, and allow it to be used for a church service, prior to the church's final decision. James readily agreed. He arrived early the next Sunday morning, helped to set up the equipment, and took his place in the second row of pews.

As James listened to the organ playing, congregational hymn singing and other preliminary activities, he began to relax. He could not quite understand the metaphor of "clinging" to the Old Rugged Cross, but readily added his voice to the chorus of that old standard for what seemed to be nine or ten verses. Despite his Catholic upbringing, James quickly dismissed – and was not readily offended by – the two or three anti-Catholic wisecracks that served as the opening humor for the pastor's sermon. He crossed his legs, allowed his shoulders to relax, leaned back, and began to look forward to the pastor's message.

The sermon, however, was targeted directly at James. It was not long before James' feet were planted firmly on the floor, his back was rigid and his forehead was showing signs of perspiration. As the pastor's voice grew louder and louder, and as the pastor began to look directly at James while he spoke, it became clear to everyone in attendance that James was the primary intended audience for the sermon that morning.

The preacher's booming declarations of the holiness of God, the sinfulness of fallen and depraved man, the terrors of Hell, and the desperate need for every sinner (and especially, in this case, James) to rely upon Jesus Christ for eternal salvation, filled the room. The sound system worked perfectly. The perspiration was beading up on James' neck as well as his forehead.

The sermon itself closely followed the content of a variety of Gospel tracts, such as "Steps to Peace with God"[2] or "Four Spiritual Laws."[3] God is holy and sinless but man (James) is not. And so, as it happens, James would burn in Hell forever unless he spoke a "sinner's prayer" accepting Jesus Christ as his personal Lord and Savior. At the conclusion of the presentation, James was presented with a simple invitation to make a simple decision about his acceptance of these truth-claims, for the sake of his eternal soul. He declined.

Later, when he was asked why he did not respond positively, or at all, to a presentation of the Gospel that offered so much (e.g., the

---

[2] *See* Billy Graham Evangelistic Association, "Steps to Peace with God," available from http://www.billygraham.org/SH_StepsToPeace.asp. Accessed 29 July 2013.
[3] *See* Campus Crusade for Christ International "Four Spiritual Laws," available from http://www.campuscrusade.com/fourlawseng.htm. Accessed 29 July 2013.

avoidance of eternal damnation) for so little (i.e., the acceptance of a few truth-claims, followed by a short confirming prayer), James offered a strange response. First, he did not find credible the idea that large, eternal consequences could be achieved with so little engagement on his part. Second, he knew that different people (and cultures, religions, and Christian denominations) had different ideas about God, so his own ideas about God (including whether or not God exists) were probably at least as credible or worthwhile as those of the pastor at the church he had visited. And he understood the Bible to be one way of understanding reality, but not necessarily the only way, and so Biblical descriptions of Hell had no meaning for him. It was all narrative. And for James, narrative-as-truth is always suspect.

Religion Made Simple

When given the opportunity, many people do choose to pray the "sinner's prayer," with the accompanying expectation that participation in this ritual will suffice to ensure their eternal salvation. This can happen at a Sunday morning service at a local church, where essential elements of the Gospel are presented in simplified terms. It can happen over coffee between two people, a proselytizer and a proselyte. It can happen in a huge football stadium or arena at a crusade that culminates in an "altar call." It can happen on the street in response to a "street evangelism" effort. And it can happen as a television viewer or a radio listener prays the special prayer in response to a broadcast invitation. Sometimes a person picks up a tract that has been left in a public place, reads through it, and makes sure to read the prayer on the last page so that the promised salvation is secured.

Many expressions of evangelical Christianity have locked onto this altar-call-plus-sinner's-prayer model of conversion. It is simple, instant and measurable. It lends itself to the glowing reports of success in the business of harvesting souls. By reducing salvation to a matter of believing four or five one-sentence doctrines, followed by the praying of a prayer of commitment, conversion becomes an individual experience that can be dated, documented, and readily referenced at any point in the future. It is also easily duplicated: with little or no training, new converts can be given bundles of tracts and set out to secure the assent of other nonbelievers. In some ways, the Great Commission (per Matthew 28:16-20) is conformed to a new pragmatism: instead of taking on the messy task of making disciples, one need only close sales.

Of course, Christianity (evangelical, fundamental, or otherwise) is not the only expression of faith that sometimes seems to offer a wide panorama of blissful eternal benefits in response to the utterance of a simple prayer or a simple credo. Islam, for example, has its *shahada*, or Declaration of the Testimony. As explained at a popular Muslim website,[4] to convert to Islam and become a Muslim, a person simply needs to pronounce, with conviction and understanding, a statement (preferably in Arabic) which acknowledges that there is no true deity except Allah and that Mohammad is a prophet of Allah. Of course, to secure all the benefits of his or her new religion, he or she will need to follow up with additional prayers and actions, but the essential conversion process, for many expressions of Islam, centers around this simple declaration.

Buddhism does not involve prayer (because it does not necessarily involve a belief in God), but does require the acceptance of some simple precepts (that is, to refrain from killing, stealing, lying, being intoxicated, and engaging in improper sexual conduct) followed by the taking of a set of three vows. These vows, often referred to as the triple gems of Buddhism, acknowledge that the convert takes refuge in the

---

[4] IslamReligion.com, at http://www.islamreligion.com/articles/204/, Accessed 29 July 2013.

5

Buddha (that is, the teacher), in the Dharma (or, the teachings), and in the Sangha (or brotherhood of Buddhists).[5]

Less formalized expressions of faith do not require even the recitation of a simple vow, declaration, or prayer. Conversion to Hinduism or to traditional Asian or African religions, tend to involve the taking up of the practices, rituals and teachings of a particular version or strain of that religion. Initiation rites are common, but because these types of religions do not require assent to absolute propositional truths, the initial conversion process is often not formalized through any particular prayer or acceptance of any particular truth-claims.

By comparison, conversion to Judaism often takes many months, and sometimes years. Requirements vary among the major groups of Judaism (Reform, Orthodox, Hasidim, etc.) but usually involve the mastery of basic Jewish ideas and practices, participation in central Jewish experiences, and a commitment to a covenantal relationship with God and with the people of the Jewish faith. In any event, a conversion to Judaism generally is not accomplished through a simple prayer of dedication.

To be fair, some expressions of Christianity are careful not to reduce the idea of conversion to the level of bumper stickers or tracts. The Roman Catholic tradition, for example, finds no particular value in the utterance of a particular prayer or vow. Instead, conversion tends to require the completion of a formalized catechesis program that usually takes several months. Adult converts are permitted to be recognized and baptized as such, but only after the required introductory formation program – as approved by the local church – and only after receiving a mandate from the local bishop.[6]

---

[5] TheBuddhaGarden.com, at http://TheBuddhaGarden.com/convert-to-buddhism.htm, Accessed 29 July 2013.

[6] International Council for Catechesis, "Adult Catechesis and the Christian Community: Some Principles and Guidelines" (Libreria Editrice Vaticana/St.

Critiques of Quick-Conversion Evangelism Techniques

Quick-conversion evangelism techniques, such as the sinner's prayer approach, have recently been the subject of concern and criticism. Patrick McIntyre, for example, has been one of the most outspoken critics of the sermon-plus-sinner's-prayer approach to evangelism. In his book, *The Graham Formula*,[7] McIntyre reviews the history of evangelism and revival techniques from the time of the Great Awakening through recent years. He claims that the evangelism and conversion process has been shortened and truncated during the 20th century. Before that time, he suggests that "evangelicals (Calvinist and Arminian) taught conversion as a definite, mystical event orchestrated by a sovereign God."[8] In other words, before the 20th century, actual conversions were rare but from McIntyre's perspective, real.

McIntyre's critique of late 20th century evangelism techniques focuses on the relative lack of counseling and follow-up. From his research, he concludes that Rev. Billy Graham never equated good altar call responses with conversions. Instead, Graham believed that even with an effective sermon, proficient counseling, and effective follow-up, only about 25% of professed decisions for Christ could be expected to have actually resulted in real conversions (that is, 25% of those who professed such decisions were likely true born-again Christians). McIntyre observes that by the end of the 20th century, evangelists (including televangelists) and preachers had reduced or eliminated any real emphasis on counseling and follow-up, to the point where the goal of revivals and evangelistic outreach meetings seemed

---

Paul Publications, 1990). Available from http://www.vatican.va/roman_curia/congregations/cclergy/documents/rc_con_cclergy_doc_14041990_acat_en.html. Accessed 29 July 2013.

[7] Patrick McIntyre, *The Graham Formula: Why most Decisions for Christ are Ineffective* (Mammoth Springs, AR: White Harvest, 2005).

[8] *Ibid*, p. 34.

merely to be to stimulate altar calls and recitations of a sinner's prayers. He concludes that under these conditions, Rev. Billy Graham's 25% conversion rate expectation (based on more optimal counseling and follow-up regimens) would be far too high.

Of course, it is dangerous to attempt any serious effort to develop empirical data about "true" versus "false" conversions. To judge whether or not someone is a sufficiently devoted follower of Christ, so as to declare that person "saved", is to pretend to see through to the heart and soul of a person in ways that can only be done by God. Nevertheless, people who do seem to have experienced a true conversion, exhibit qualities ("fruits of the spirit," in Pauline terms, as seen at Galatians 5:16-26 and elsewhere), and those qualities, habits and virtues tend to reveal a changed person. From this perspective, it is not inappropriate or unfair to question the genuineness of conversions of those who respond to alter calls or otherwise acknowledge having prayed the sinner's prayer, but whose lives do not reflect long-term changes in personal behavior.

Many observers, including both religious and secular researchers, have commented about the relatively small percentage of such "converts" who seem to have emerged from the conversion experience as true disciples of Jesus Christ. Sociologist Donald Miller, for example, conducted a study of certain Christian groups, including Calvary Chapel, Vineyard Christian Fellowship, and Hope Chapel.[9] He paid careful attention to the entrepreneurial aspects of these organizations and efforts. Although Miller acknowledged the growth and marketing effectiveness of these organizations, he also observed that only a few "recruits" who made professions of faith showed evidence of radical or long-term spirituality. Miller noted, for example, that the staff of the Horizon Christian Fellowship in Costa Mesa, California estimated

---

[9] Donald E. Miller, *Reinventing American Protestantism: Christianity in the New Millennium* (Berkely, CA: University of California Press, 1997).

that 16,000 conversions occurred at their site in the five-year period from 1986 to 1991 but that only 10% of these decisions resulted in long-term changes in personal behavior.[10]

This book is not an attempt to fix this conversion erosion. However, assuming that McIntyre is correct, and that the missing ingredients are counseling and follow-up, this book could be viewed as an inquiry into the content of such interaction and discourse. What kinds of issues should be addressed? What kind of questions should be asked? What should the counselor/proselytizer know about the frustrations typically experienced by those who are seeking meaning and purpose in life? How can these frustrations be empathetically discussed with the counselee/proselyte, in preparation for a sober and honest inquiry into the Gospel?

In his critique of 20th century conversion erosion, McIntyre does not delve into these questions. He does point to Jonathan Edwards' eight stages of salvation, described by Erroll Hulse[11] as being especially instructive. Edwards emphasized, as a precondition for salvation, the importance of "an awakening to danger, a sense of horror at being eternally lost," and a conviction that the natural state of the unsaved soul is one of "extreme wretchedness and misery."[12] McIntyre also points to the role of the local church in helping new converts better understand their faith, and appreciate both the need for ongoing and continual self-examination, as well as the various ways in which they can observe how God is changing them as they grow in their faith.[13]

Such an appreciation for the importance of counseling and personal interaction over time, in the conversion process, did not originate with

---

[10] *Ibid*, pp. 172-173.

[11] McIntyre, *The Graham Formula*, at p. 37, *citing* Erroll Hulse, *The Great Invitation: Examining the Use of the Invitation System in Evangelism*. (Welwyn: Evangelical, 1986).

[12] *Ibid*.

[13] *Ibid*, p. 105.

McIntyre. In a well-known study that included Catholics, Anglicans, Methodists, Baptists and other expressions of Christianity, researcher John Finney observed that a common factor associated with obvious and long-term conversions is connectedness to a local church.[14] He is often attributed with having developed the notion of "community before conversion." That is, his research seems to indicate that "true" conversions happen most often after a proselyte has been incorporated into some kind of communal experience with believers, rather than before. In contrast, the revival-meeting paradigm, as critiqued by McIntyre, tends to emphasize on-the-spot conversion, followed by an intentional effort to "plug" the newly-professing believer into a local church. Finney's research seems to indicate that the former methodology is more effective than the latter, and his work has formed the basis for Alpha, Emmaus, Christianity Explored, and other 12- to 15-week small-group programs designed to aid nonbelievers in their journey toward faith.[15]

Empathic Pre-Evangelism

Despite the concerns expressed above about over-simplifying the Gospel, this book does not quarrel with, or even question, the truth-claims of the Gospel, even as presented in the most basic and simplified fashion. After all, nothing in the widely used Gospel tracts (such as "Four Spiritual Laws") is so inconsistent with the Bible as to be considered untrue or heretical.

Nor does this book deny the possibility that even the most succinct or abstracted articulation of the truth-claims of the Gospel in a tract,

---

[14] John Finney, *Finding Faith Today* (Swindon, UK: British and Foreign Bible Society, 1992).

[15] *See* Booker, Mike, and Mark Ireland. *Evangelism – Which Way Now?: An Evaluation of Alpha, Emmaus, Cell Church and Other Contemporary Strategies for Evangelism* (London: Church House, 2003), pp. 4-9.

a sermon, a website, or any other type of presentation of any length, can contain sufficient information so as to allow a person to become a follower of Jesus Christ or to reject Christ (and to be found responsible for having done so). Indeed, the Holy Spirit can use much less than even these types of abbreviated explanations in order to prompt a person to recognize — and accept or reject — his or her desperate need for a relationship with Jesus Christ based on His Person and His work at the Cross and grave.

Instead, this book asks whether it might make sense under some circumstances – especially in one-on-one conversations between a believer and a nonbeliever – for the evangelizer to take into account, and attend to, the somewhat post-modern perspective that the nonbeliever might be bringing with him or her into the discourse. Some nonbelievers, for example, do not have a very large or robust or clear sense of God's existence and holiness, and will resist a Gospel presentation that starts with and builds upon the fundamental idea of a holy and just God. If a nonbeliever is cynical toward such meta-narratives as the Bible, or is generally skeptical about truth-claims pertaining to right and wrong, it might not make sense to simply assert that he or she is a sinner deserving of Hell because the Bible says so. Eventually, the nonbeliever will need to understand and face these claims in order to accept or reject the Gospel of Jesus Christ.

The question behind this book is: What is the best way to get them to that point? Specifically, should presentations of the Gospel necessarily begin with text-based truth-claims? Many nonbelievers – and especially those post-modern nonbelievers who are skeptical of sacred texts and moral claims – carry around a burden of doubts and anxieties about life. How can the Gospel be introduced in such a way that it addresses these kinds of existential doubts and anxieties?

An Apologetic Sidebar for Post-Moderns?

Most systematic approaches to theology proper, as well as to apologetics, build on basic or foundational truth-claims in order to propose or defend more specific Gospel-related truth-claims. If, for example, it can be shown that, based on the weight of biblical and extra-biblical evidence, the resurrection of Jesus Christ is a reasonable and believable truth-claim, the deity of Christ can be held out to also be a reasonable and believable truth-claim. Once the deity of Jesus Christ is reasonably established, the plausibility of the virgin birth, the miracles performed by Christ, and the veracity of his statements can be established. At this point, the specific claims of the Gospel can be proffered in a way that is coherent and that corresponds to the previously established truth-claims. This evidentiary approach to apologetics begins with empirical evidence and ends with Gospel truth-claims.[16]

Similarly, classical Reformed epistemology apologists, who emphasize the natural knowledge of God that He has implanted within us (and who do not emphasize a need for empirical evidence), build their more specific arguments upon more generalized foundations. The compelling and coherent narratives of Scripture regarding God, creation, the sin of Adam and Eve and the corresponding need for redemption, form the basis for the specifics of the Gospel. There is within this approach a confidence in the ability of humans to grasp (or recognize) the foundational truths as presented in the Bible. From this perspective, culpability for non-acceptance (or non-recognition) of Jesus Christ as Lord and Savior is premised, at least in part, upon

---

[16] *See, e.g.,* Gary R. Habermas and Mike Licona, *The Case for the Resurrection of Jesus* (Grand Rapids, MI: Kregel Publications, 2004), which makes the case for evidentiary apologetics.

the presupposition that nonbelievers have rejected these Biblical truth-claims.

But the acceptance of truth-claims generally, and faith-based truth-claims in particular, is problematic in this 21st century. Adherents to religious views, Christian or otherwise, are often thought of as being narrow-minded, if not outright ignorant. Many people today are predisposed to believe that truth-claims are necessarily subjective, culturally-informed, impermanent and bound up within language that is itself infected with bias and subjectivity. The usefulness of the law of non-contradiction is largely viewed as being limited to verifiable (and some mathematical) propositions, such as the proposition that the earth is not flat (Thomas L. Friedman notwithstanding[17]), but does not (and cannot possibly) extend to metaphysical assertions.

Skepticism, even radical skepticism, is not new, of course. But the pervasiveness of skepticism in the latter half of the 20th century was noteworthy. The general loss of idealism about the expectation that science and technology would somehow solve the major problems of mankind (such idealism having been generally proven delusional in view of the Holocaust, the development of nuclear and biological weapons, and the failure to solve the problems of poverty and human depravity) came to be known as the "post-modern condition."[18]

Prior to the coinage of the term "post-modern," Francis A. Schaeffer used the term "twentieth-century man" to identify that group of people for whom absolutes do not exist. Schaeffer saw the Western population at large as being generally divided into two groups: "modern man," for whom truth and rationality still hold meaning and sway, and

---

[17] *See* Thomas L. Friedman, *The World Is Flat: A Brief History of the Twenty-First Century* (New York: Farrar, Straus and Giroux, 2006), explaining the effective "flattening" of the world as a result of the internet, telecommunications, global economics, and world travel.

[18] This phenomenon of post-modernism is discussed in greater detail *infra* at the end of Chapter 2.

"twentieth-century man," for whom these foundations generally do not hold meaning. His deep concern was that the language, concepts and propositions put forth by the evangelical church at the end of the 20th century only seemed to speak to the former pool of prospective believers. No real connection was being made to the latter pool of proselytes, largely because the words, presumptions, and truth-claims of evangelists did not have meaning. Their skepticism ran too deep.[19] And, as Ronald B. Mayers observed, the "hermeneutical gap" between the two poles "will most likely grow wider, and thus the apologetic link will have to be more intimate and personal."[20]

There are, of course, plenty of apologetics resources available today to assist in rebutting the notion of radical skepticism, and to disabuse people of many of the tenets associated with post-modernism. But why should anyone be interested in hearing such arguments? What would motivate a self-satisfied post-modern skeptic to seriously consider even the most preliminary, foundational truth-claims that underpin the Gospel? After all, it is quite easy for someone to casually dismiss, as being subjective and merely hypothetical, truth-claims made by anyone, not to mention followers of Christ. Agnosticism is easier to defend than atheism, and nihilism calls for no defense at all.

The answer to these questions is simple: it falls to the evangelist to disrupt the *status quo* of the nonbeliever and to provide a reality hook that will allow the Gospel to have meaning and significance. This has always been the case. The ministry of Jesus Christ is replete with examples of paradigms being imploded, human-derived presuppositions being exposed for their inconsistencies and lack of coherence, and

[19] Francis A. Schaeffer, *The Church at the End of the Twentieth Century; Including, The Church Before the Watching World* (Wheaton, Ill: Crossway Books, 1994), pp. 50-53.
[20] Ronald B. Mayers, *Balanced Apologetics: Using Evidences and Presuppositions in Defense of the Faith* (Grand Rapids, MI: Kregel Publications, 1996), p. 8.

idolatrous worldviews being brushed aside. The Areopagus speech of Paul the apostle follows this model, as he undermined many of the religious presumptions of the leaders who were gathered there to hear him. Indeed, many of the graphic descriptions of the torments of Hell brought forth by writers, preachers, painters and playwrights over the last two millennia have often had as their purpose the intention of shaking people loose from their dangerous contentedness.

The primary difference between traditional efforts at bringing the "fear of God" to the attention of a proselyte, and what is being considered as part of this book, is the point at which this type of disruptive, presumption-shattering discourse takes place. Traditionally, discussions of Hell and eternal separation from God are appropriate as part of an overall discussion of the consequences of sin and the need for redemption. But for many conversations with people who have a post-modern perspective, much groundwork needs to be laid before a discussion of the specific claims of the Gospel makes sense. Instead of starting with a discussion of the consequences of the eternal separation from God (with a person who is unsure about whether God exists, or even whether truth exists), this work considers whether it makes sense to first attend to the general fear of the unknown, and the generalized anxiety about the possibility of future nothingness that can, and often does, accompany belief systems that include atheism, agnosticism, radical skepticism, radical relativism, and nihilism.

Take, for example, the work of Norman L. Geisler and Frank Turek, entitled *I Don't Have Enough Faith to Be an Atheist*.[21] This book lays out a pathway of argumentation that starts with questions about whether truth exists (Chapter 1), and whether reasonable belief in truth-claims can ever make sense (Chapter 2). The authors then proceed through thirteen chapters of traditional apologetics pertaining

---

[21] Norman L. Geisler and Frank Turek, *I Don't Have Enough Faith to Be an Atheist* (Wheaton, Ill: Crossway Books, 2004).

to intelligent design, the fine-tuning of creation enabling the sustenance of life, the problem of evil, the reliability of the Bible, the evidence of the resurrection, the deity and credibility of Jesus Christ, and other important arguments. The book lays the groundwork for a properly vetted presentation of the compelling claims of the Gospel.

Following this outline, a traditional presentation of the essential principles of salvation through faith in Jesus Christ would make complete sense somewhere around Chapter 13, where the authors make the case that Jesus is God. It is at this point that a discussion of the holiness of God, the sinfulness of man, and the need for propitiation through Jesus Christ, can make sense. It is also at this point that an appropriate discussion of the consequences of sin, including a proper recognition of the significance of eternal damnation, becomes not only important, but reasonable and appropriate.

This book would not propose to change any of the steps, arguments, or apologetic discussions set forth by Geisler and Turek. Instead, it is suggested that the traditional apologetic pathway to the Cross might be supplemented, perhaps at Chapter 2 of *I Don't Have Enough Faith to Be an Athiest*, with some additional considerations about the phenomenon of dread. As it happens, Geisler and Turek do point to the work of James W. Sire, who suggests that people believe what they believe, in part, because their belief systems often give them psychological comfort and peace of mind (especially in regard to meaning and purpose in life).[22] Sire refers to these beneficial outcomes as psychological reasons for belief. But neither Geisler and Turek, nor Sire, make the connection between the post-modern condition of radical skepticism and the experience of a loss of these psychological reasons for belief. In other words, these authors seem to miss the opportunity to propose that

---

[22] *See* James W. Sire, *Why Should Anyone Believe Anything at All?* (Downers Grove, Ill: InterVarsity Press, 1994). Geisler and Turek refer both to Sire's book, and to his college seminars of the same name.

once post-modern skepticism settles in, there is a diminution or loss of beliefs; this results in a painful loss of peace of mind, which, in turn, can trigger a fresh inquiry into meta-narratives and worldviews.[23]

In Chapter 2 of their work, Geisler and Turek offer logical arguments for reconstructing basic foundations for truth. They do this by explaining the law of non-contradiction, and by critiquing the skepticism of David Hume and the agnosticism of Immanuel Kant. They also point out that truths about God can be known, and that a refusal to consider such truths can have eternal consequences.

What is missing in this presentation by Geisler and Turek, is a "reality hook." That is, except for those persons who might be deeply concerned about the reliability of their worldview, there is no compelling, gut-level disturbance created by the concerns raised in Chapter 2 of Geisler and Turek's work. But there could be. If a person has adopted a philosophical perspective that offers no reasonable or reliable explanation of purpose in life or meaning in life, that person is likely to experience some level of existential dread, i.e., some anxiety about the unknown and unknowable being-in-nothingness that results from, say, the skepticism of Hume or the agnosticism of Kant. This book represents an effort to flesh out the phenomenon of existential dread and to consider its significance in the context of conversational evangelism.

A Deep, Troubling Concern about the Eternal Unknown

Any presentation of the Gospel that avoids a discussion of Hell also avoids a possible connection to the nonbeliever's natural concern about what happens after death. On the other hand, a description and discussion of Hell – as an opening volley in a Gospel presentation – is

---

[23] The psychological discomfort arising from a lack of a robust web of beliefs, as alluded to by Sire, is addressed in the next chapter of this dissertation.

not necessarily the same as a discourse that takes into account the anxieties that come from considering the possible emptiness (or worse) that occurs after death. Some people who might recoil at — and who might reject out of hand — suggestions of eternal punishment in a lake of fire based on descriptions in the Bible, are not at peace with the prospect of death. And they are not necessarily comfortable about the possibility of being held to account, after death, for their life on this earth.

And so, this book considers whether there can be a natural progression toward a presentation of the truth-claims of the Gospel that ends with text but does not necessarily start with text. It can start instead with empathy toward nonbelievers who carry with them the burden of life's deeper anxieties, those for whom life has become shallow, boring, and troubling: those for whom life is not making sense.

Many nonbelievers (including those who might be considered post-moderns) are essentially radical skeptics who would deny the existence of absolute truth. Before they can reasonably be expected to grasp the possibility of the propositional truth-claims of the Gospel, it may be necessary to first move them toward the possibility of moral truth or truth itself. This is consistent with the notion of *pre-evangelism* as articulated by Norman L. and David Geisler. In *Conversational Evangelism*, the authors defined pre-evangelism as "tilling the soil of people's minds and hearts to help them be more willing to listen to the truth."[24] From a practical viewpoint, this book extends the work of the Geislers by suggesting that the experience of existential dread is a common, if not universal, phenomenon and that conversational evangelism might include an exploration of the implications of that phenomenon.

---

[24] Geisler, Norman L., and David Geisler. *Conversational Evangelism* (Eugene, Or: Harvest House Publishers, 2009), p. 22.

Individuals who are experiencing such existential dread may need some help transitioning from their experience to the Gospel's explanation. They may have big questions to ask, and those questions may anticipate more than a few simple fact statements drawn from the Bible. Even if it is true that, as the bumper sticker declares, "Jesus is the answer," it may take some work before the *angst*-laden individual can fully appreciate how true that aphorism really is. It may take some effort to help the nonbeliever appreciate his or her own desire to know, as Miguel de Unamuno suggests, "not so much the 'why' as the 'wherefore,' not the cause but the end."[25]

Conversing with the Heart

It is often said that to speak to a person about the anxieties of life, and about the larger, looming questions of life and death, is to speak "to their heart." This idea of "speaking to the heart" is a colloquialism that has a long history. As Christian D. Ginsburg observed in his 1861 commentary on the book of Ecclesiastes, the heart has historically been regarded among the Hebrews and other nations, not only as the seat of the passions, but also as possessing the faculty of thinking, judging, etc.[26] Ginsberg points to Cicero and several other ancient and classical writers, as well as to passages from the Bible. He notes, for example, how the writer of Ecclesiastes speaks to his heart (Ecclesiastes 2:20),

[25] Miguel de Unamuno, *The Tragic Sense of Life in Men and Nations*. Trans. Anthony Kerrigan. Ed. Anthony Kerrigan and Martin Nozick. Bollingen Series 85, no. 4 (Princeton, N.J.: Princeton University Press, 1972), p. 24.

[26] Christian David Ginsburg, *The Song of Songs and Coheleth (Commonly Called The Book of Ecclesiastes)*. (New York: KTVA Publ. House, 1970). Available from http://www.archive.org/stream/cohelethcommonly00ginsuoft/cohelethcommonly00ginsuoft_djvu.txt
Accessed 29 July 2013. Person-heart discourse is also alluded to in the New Testament, but not as directly or as metaphorically.

directs his heart (Ecclesiastes 2:20), and communes with his heart (Ecclesiastes 1:16).

In the New Testament, similarly, the heart is associated with the acquisition of belief and of faith. In Romans 10:10, we are told "it is with your heart that you believe." And in Romans 10:6, Paul quotes from Deuteronomy 30:12 when he uses the expression, 'do not say in your heart, "who will ascend into heaven?"' The heart is also identified by Jesus Christ at Matthew 15:18 and at Luke 6:45 as the source of words and thoughts. This is similar to the expression in Psalm 15:2 "[He] who speaks truth from his heart," and in Psalm 49:3 "My mouth will speak words of wisdom; the utterance from my heart will give understanding."

This appreciation for the role of the heart in acquiring beliefs and in holding knowledge has continued throughout history. In the traditional, post-Enlightenment articulation of what it means to understand, and to convert to, Christianity, there has been tension between an emphasis on the heart, on the one hand, and an emphasis on the head, on the other. The former is associated with the passions, inclinations, and affections: the latter, with knowledge and with clarity of understanding.

The terminology used to describe this tension can often be confusing. Some, like Jonathan Edwards, described the "soul" in terms of two faculties: cognition and intention. Edwards differentiates between these two faculties in *Religious Affections*:

> God has indued the soul with two faculties: one is that by which it is capable of perception and speculation, or by which it discerns, and views, and judges of things; which is called the understanding. The other faculty is that by which the soul does not merely perceive and view things, but is some way inclined with respect to

the things it views or considers; either is inclined to them, or is disinclined and averse from them; or is the faculty by which the soul does not behold things, as an indifferent unaffected spectator, but either as liking or disliking, pleased or displeased, approving or rejecting. This faculty is called by various names; it is sometimes called the inclination: and, as it has respect to the actions that are determined and governed by it, is called the *will*: and the mind, with regard to the exercises of this faculty, is often called the *heart* [Emphasis in original].[27]

For Edwards, any meaningful and efficacious knowledge of God, and of the Gospel, requires, and is contingent upon, the exercise of the mind as well as the heart. A mere understanding of the truth-claims of the Gospel, and a cognitive assent to those truth-claims, is insufficient for a true conversion to Christianity.

Indeed, Edwards' understanding of the essence of such a conversion involves "a new heart, a new sense and inclination that is a principle of new life, a principle that, however small, is active and has a vigor and power and as it more beats and struggles, thirsts after holiness, aims at and tends to everything that belongs to the new creature, and has within it the foundation and source of the whole."[28] This appreciation for a new heart at the time of conversion is, for Edwards, anticipated by and consistent with, Ezekiel 36:26,27: "I will give you a new heart

---

[27] Jonathan Edwards, *Religious Affections*, vol. 2 of *The Works of Jonathan Edwards*, ed. John E. Smith (New Haven: Yale University Press, 1959), p. 96. Available from http://www.leaderu.com/cyber/books/religaffect/rapt1sec1.html Accessed 29 July 2013.

[28] Jonathan Edwards, *Images or Shadows of Divine Things*, in *Typological Writings*, vol. 11 of *The Works of Jonathan Edwards*, ed. by Wallace E. Anderson (New Haven: Yale University Press, 1948) no. 190: pp. 122-123.

and put a new spirit in you; I will remove from you your heart of stone and give you a heart of flesh. And I will put my Spirit in you and move you to follow my decrees and be careful to keep my laws."[29]

Of course, Edwards had his detractors. As a leader of a group of "rationalists", Charles Chauncy, a minister at the First Church in Boston, objected to Edwards' emphasis on the heart. He was concerned that this emphasis led ministers to abandon their congregations in favor of itinerant ministries, which resulted in a lack of such disciplines as daily devotions and diligent work, and led to inappropriate expressions of religious fervor like screaming and wanton emotionalism. He insisted that an enlightened mind rather than elevated affections should govern both one's religious and one's secular demeanor and behavior.[30]

The concern about the influence and involvement of the heart also mirrors a rationalistic bias that is often associated with the Enlightenment. During the Enlightenment, reason was elevated above revelation, and in the process, revelation was associated with "the heart" as opposed to "the mind". As Henry F. May has observed, "Men of the Enlightenment agreed that divine revelation could not establish truths which were contrary to reason."[31]

Some have suggested that evangelical preachers, including Jonathan Edwards and others associated with the Great Awakening, responded to the Enlightenment attack on revelation and faith by overemphasizing the heart and its relationship to belief.[32] However true this allegation

[29] *See* Jonathan Edwards, *Treatise on Grace*, ed. Paul Helm (Cambridge: James Clark, 1971),pp. 55-56. Available from http://www.dailybread.com.au/5000/200/202/Jonathan_Edwards/Treatise%20on%20Grace.pdf Accessed 29 July 2013.
[30] Conrad Cherry, *The Theology of Jonathan Edwards: A Reappraisal* (New York: Doubleday and Company, Inc., 1966), pp. 165-167.
[31] Henry F. May. *The Enlightenment In America*. (London: Oxford University Press, 1976; Oxford Press, 1978), p. xiv.
[32] *See* James Turner. *Without God, Without Creed*. (Baltimore: The John Hopkins University, 1985) at p. 110 ("[M]any ministers by 1850 preached as if emotion itself

may have been, there continues to exist today a tension between the idea of "heart knowledge" (with an emphasis on worship, zeal, and emotional devotion) and "head knowledge" (with an emphasis on scholarly hermeneutics and rigorous apologetics).

Restless Hearts in the 21ˢᵗ Century

Saint Augustine wrote that his heart was restless, and that restlessness eventually prompted him to find rest in Jesus Christ.[33] This book is about that restlessness, i.e., that sense of uneasiness that afflicts the human experience, and that has been described, addressed, or explored in literature, philosophy, and psychology, among other sources. As a shorthand reference to that restlessness, the term "dread" will be used, and this notion of dread will be unpacked and analyzed in the next few chapters. This book will investigate such questions as: What is that restlessness like? How has it been recognized and addressed by philosophers, psychologists, and others? How can a believer empathize with that restlessness, as part of an effort to help the unbeliever appreciate the great hope that the Gospel offers?[34] How can the Gospel be introduced so that it dazzles gradually? (Before the

verified God.") and at p. 198 (". . . to more and more people, belief in God seemed to express feeling rather than to state knowledge.").

[33] *See* Saint Augustine, *Confessions,* trans. Edward Bouverie Pusey (New York: Book of the Month Club, 1996), 1 ("Thou made us for Thyself, and our heart is restless, until it repose in Thee."). Also available from http://www.classicreader.com/book/1738/1/. Accessed 29 July 2013

[34] I am not proposing here that simple, tract-level presentations of the Gospel be eliminated. If a preacher, or evangelist, or any other believer, is convinced that they ought to be presenting the "Four Spiritual Laws" or a similar articulation of the Gospel at a given time or place or circumstance, I am not suggesting otherwise. But what is being considered here is the possible role that a greater empathy and awareness of the nature of an unbeliever's existential dread might play in the evangelism process.

second and third question can be answered, the answer to the first must be known: How can the human sense of restlessness be adequately described?)

The awkwardness of dread-consciousness has been articulated in recent years by the existentialists of the 20th century. Atheists and fellow travelers Jean Paul Sartre and Albert Camus expressed many of the same sentiments as did Søren Kierkegaard (1813-1855) and Miguel de Unamuno. -de Unamuno, in particular, put his finger on the *angst* of consciousness by calling it a tragic sense of life, and a disease:

> There is something which, for want of a better name, we shall call the tragic sense of life, and it carries along with it an entire conception of the Universe and of life itself, an entire philosophy more or less formulated, more or less conscious. In this sense may animate, and does animate, not only individual men, but entire peoples... And it is no good talking, as we shall see, of men sound and unsound. Apart from the fact that there is no normal standard of health, no one has ever proved that man must necessarily be joyful by nature. But there is more to it than that: man, because he is man, because he possesses consciousness, is already, in comparison to the jackass or the crab, a sick animal. Consciousness is a disease.[35]

In fact, de Unamuno calls this disease – this debilitating yearning to achieve coherence in regard to all of life – "one that arouses in us the

---

[35] de Unamuno, *Tragic Sense of Life*, pp. 21-22.

appetite to know for the sole pleasure of knowing, the delight of tasting the fruit of the Tree of Knowledge of Good and Evil."[36]

And so we are using the term "dread" here to refer to the somewhat vague and gnawing anxiety about the possibility of the meaninglessness of life. This anxiety is often heightened or made more obvious when we think about (or are faced with) our own death. A sense of guilt or feelings of shame can also intensify this experience of dread, or make it more obvious. Unlike the efforts of Tillich[37] and others, this work will not attempt to draw clear lines of differentiation between anxiety about death, anxiety about guilt, and anxiety about the meaninglessness of life. Instead, anxiety about meaninglessness is treated as being a sufficient characterization of the "object" of the generalized dread for purposes of this discussion.

Even as we have defined it here, there is an elusiveness about dread. It is experienced, but it is not understood. It prompts thoughtfulness and self-reflection, but is seldom sated by any particular conclusions or any level of new found coherence. In some ways it is an emotion, and in some ways it represents an intellectual query. As Blaise Pascal once said, "the heart has its reasons of which reason knows nothing."[38] Dread also has its reasons, of which reason knows nothing.

---

[36] *Ibid*, p. 25. de Unamuno's reference is, of course, to Genesis 3, wherein the idol of autonomous, rationalized, godless moral authority, is sought by Adam and Eve in disobedience and in lieu of their reliance upon the moral truth made available to them directly from God.

[37] *See* Tillich, Paul. *The Courage to Be.* (New Haven: Yale University Press, 1952). Tillich suggested that a generalized anxiety about death or imminent nothingness was the dominant concern in antiquity; that anxiety about guilt characterized the transition from the medieval period to the Reformation; and that anxiety about meaninglessness *per se* is best associated with the end of modernism. By comparison, this work does not rely on these distinctions.

[38] Blaise Pascal and A. J. Krailsheimer. *Pensées*, #423 (London: Penguin Books, 1995), p. 127.

2

EXISTENTIAL DREAD AND THE PHILOSOPHICAL SEARCH FOR MEANING

Animals learn death first at the moment of death;... man approaches death with the knowledge it is closer every hour, and this creates a feeling of uncertainty over his life, even for him who forgets in the business of life that annihilation is awaiting him. It is for this reason chiefly that we have philosophy and religion.

Arthur Schopenhauer[39]

---

[39] Arthur Schopenhauer and Eric Francis Jules Payne. [*Die Welt Als Wille Und Vorstellung.*] *The World As Will and Representation, Volume II,* Translated by E.F.J. Payne (New York: Dover, 1966), p. 463.

Philosophical Despair as a Condition

Jacques Maritain (1882-1973) had been born and raised in Paris. His father was a non-practicing Catholic, and his mother was a liberal, mostly secular, Protestant. He grew up without personal religious faith. In his late teens, he wrestled with questions about life's meaning, and did not find answers in any of his studies. There was nothing transcendental, or enchanting, or spiritually engaging about the materialism and nominalism that informed the teachers and educators of his youth.

When it came time for Jacques to attend university, he enrolled at the Sorbonne. There, he met a young Jewish girl, Raïssa Oumansoff, who was also disillusioned by the inability of empirical science and analytical philosophy to provide answers for life's meaning. One day, as the couple walked hand-in-hand in a Paris park, they made a pact that they would commit suicide if, within a year, they could not find any meaning to life beyond the material.[40]

Maritain's experience was not unique. In fact, it resembles the intellectual inquiries that have been made by philosophers and other thinkers throughout recorded history. In this chapter, the endpoints of philosophical inquiry, especially in the Western tradition, starting with Greco-Roman philosophers and ending with recent existential philosophers, will be considered (along with some acknowledgment of the general flow of philosophical threads throughout the intervening millennia). This is not intended to be a comprehensive survey of the intellectual history of Western philosophy. Instead, this discussion is intended to show how larger questions about life, and the meaning of

---

[40] Julie Kernan, *Our Friend, Jacques Maritain: A Personal Memoir* (Garden City, N.Y.: Doubleday, 1975), pp. 15-25. The couple did not commit suicide. In fact, shortly after they were married, they found meaning in the Catholic faith. Jacques, in particular, went on to become a well-known Thomist philosopher.

life, have been asked and engaged over time. The questions that were asked in ancient Athens are essentially the same questions that are being asked today. To some extent, they were the questions that Jacques and Raïssa asked during their college years.

Is It Enough to Seek Meaning?

To Be Human, Is to Ask What it Means to Be Human

The historical record of the human experience is cluttered with question marks. Philosophers, religious leaders, storytellers, soothsayers, and, more recently, psychologists, have taken their turns posing questions about the meaning of life and, many times, offering possible answers.[41] Seldom have those proposed answers satisfied the human longing for hope and meaning.

Socrates (469-399 BC), the ancient Greek philosopher, has served for centuries as the embodiment of the human search for meaning. Most of what we know about Socrates comes to us by way of Plato (427-348 BC), who founded the school in Athens known as the Academy. Among the writings of Plato are the *Dialogues*, a series of discussions and arguments between Socrates and various others (many of whom represented the perspectives of schools of philosophies other than that of Socrates, such as the Sophists).

As Plato reveals in the *Apology*, Socrates declared – immediately before he was sentenced to death – that "the unexamined life is not worth living for a human being" (38a).[42] In other words, for Socrates,

---

[41] *See, e.g.,* Allen Diogenes and Eric O. Springsted. *Philosophy for Understanding Theology,* 2nd ed. (Louisville, London: Westminster John Knox Press, 2007*)*; and David Benatar, *Life, Death & Meaning: Key Philosophical Readings on the Big Questions* (Lanham, Maryland: Rowman & Littlefield Publishers, 2004).

[42] Plato, "Apology of Socrates," in Thomas G. West and Grace Starry West, trans., *Four Texts on Socrates: Plato's Euthyphro, Apology, and Crito and Aristophanes' Clouds*

the ultimate purpose of life is to be engaged in seeking the ultimate purpose in life. Since we are hardwired to be concerned about the meaning and purpose in our life, Socrates concluded that a life that does not involve the embracing of these larger questions is a life hardly worth living. Animals don't seem to be concerned about purpose in life, and when human beings abandon themselves to a life of mere existence, perhaps seeking comfort and pleasure but little else, their existence approaches that of animals.

When Socrates made this declaration about the unexamined life, he was, in a sense, pleading for his own life. But not persuasively, and perhaps not wholeheartedly. He was, at the time, appearing in court to defend himself from a set of charges brought forth by several prominent Athenian accusers, including Meletus, Anytus, and Lycon. The charges included allegations that Socrates was "guilty of corrupting the minds of the young, and of believing in deities of his own invention instead of the gods recognized by the state" (24b).[43] In particular, Socrates was accused of suggesting that the Greek gods could be measured by an ultimate standard of right and wrong, and that reason can lead to the discovery of moral principles against which the deities could be judged. This made his practice of reasoning and questioning intolerable for the Athenian accusers and political leaders.

Socrates, in turn, concluded that if he were to give up his role as a questioner and meaning-seeker, while living in Athens, life would not be worth living, even if he were allowed to practice his craft of philosophizing. And he also concluded that if he were exiled from Athens, life would also not be worth living. So a more accurate statement might have been, that the unexamined life in Athens, or any kind of life outside of Athens, is not worth living.

For Socrates, philosophical inquiry was the final cause of human

(Ithaca, NY: Cornell University Press, 1984), p. 92.
[43] *Ibid*, p. 73.

existence: that is, it was the cosmic purpose of life (or, at least, of his life). This presumption was consistent with the general notion of his day that everything must have a purpose. Inherent within this presumption was the teleological expectation that there was somehow a larger plan or purpose for all of reality. When Socrates found himself facing deprivation of that which he believed to be his place within this larger purpose, he could not see the point of living any longer.[44] Purposefulness was, for Socrates, a requirement for life.

To Ask What it Means to Be Human, Is to Inquire about Death

An interesting feature of Socrates' life-as-an-inquiry proposition is that philosophical inquiry inevitably leads to questions about death. It is impossible to ask about the meaning of life, without taking into account the looming prospect of inevitable death. Questions about death must necessarily be included in any serious investigation of the meaning of life.

This necessity of taking death into account as part of any meaningful inquiry about life, was acknowledged by Socrates, and most noticeably articulated in Plato's *Phaedo*. There, Socrates is quoted as saying that "all who apply themselves to the study of philosophy aright are, unknown to the rest of the world, as far as depends on themselves, engaged in nothing else than in studying the art of dying

---

[44] As Stace observed, belief in final causes amounted to a belief that the world is governed by purposes, presumably the purposes of some overruling mind. This belief is not the invention of Christianity, but was basic to the whole of Western civilization from the time of Socrates to the rise of science in 17th century. Walter T. Stace, "Man Against Darkness," in *The Meaning of Life: Questions, Answers, and Analysis*, edited by Steven Sanders and David R. Cheney (Englewood Cliffs, N.J.: Prentice-Hall, 1980), p. 39.

and death" [69b].[45] Socrates also believed that life after death would be pleasant for those whose lives were engaged in higher pursuits. In the *Phaedo*, immediately prior to the passage quoted above, Socrates acknowledged that it seemed reasonable to him that a person "who has really spent his life in the pursuit of philosophy should be cheerful in the near prospect of death, and a sure hold after death of obtaining in another world the highest blessings" [69a].[46]

Socrates did not appear to be especially troubled by this connection of philosophical inquiry to death and mortality. In part, this was because for him philosophy itself, rather than the conclusions to which it might lead, was the highest purpose or calling for the individual. It was also because, despite the accusations of the Athenian elders, Socrates was not a materialist. He believed in the immortality of the soul and in an afterlife.

Socrates' beliefs about the immortality of the soul flowed from his understanding of philosophy-as-preparation-for-death. In other words, the very fact that philosophical inquiry naturally triggers a thoughtfulness and a curiosity about beginnings and endings, birth and death, and the extension of time beyond the span of one's life experience, convinced Socrates that there must be a reality beyond time, space, and materiality. To ignore the metaphysical was tantamount to choosing ignorance. Ignorance, in turn, was tantamount to sin.

But ignorance was not, in Socrates' view, the only sin. Socrates' sense of transcendence included a robust morality. In the concluding remarks of his apology, Socrates points out that the worst fate that a human being could endure would be to do evil. Among his last words to the judges who had condemned him to death were the following:

---

[45] Plato, *Plato's Phaedo: Literally Translated.* Trans. Edward Meredith Cope. (Cambridge: University Press, 1875), p. 14.
[46] *Ibid.*

But you too, judges, should be of good hope toward death, and you should think this one thing to be true: that there is nothing bad for a good man, whether living or dead, and that the gods are not without care for his troubles [41c].[47]

The Problem with Meaning-Seeking as the Highest Good

Meaning-seeking as a means to an end is a critical and essential part of life's experience. The human need to seek purpose and meaning in life seems to be hardwired. Eternity does in fact seem to have been planted in the human heart (Ecclesiastes 3:11).[48]

Meaning-seeking as a response to philosophical despair is, in fact, the premise and the theme of this work. If there can be a trigger that will prompt an individual to seek meaning in life, the individual will be more open and more prepared to receive and accept the truth-claims of the Gospel than he would otherwise. And if existential dread serves as that trigger, the dread is itself a gift that can prompt a person to travel a pathway to an even greater Gift.

But meaning-seeking for its own sake is unsatisfying, Socrates' suicide notwithstanding. After all, Socrates did not declare on the eve of his death that the self-examined life is necessarily worth living. He only proclaimed that the unexamined life is not worth living. To the extent that a refusal to consider one's purpose in life would preclude any inquiry into such larger questions as the existence of God, whether there is life after death, whether there is an accountability for one's ethical choices, etc., Socrates was probably correct. The unexamined life may indeed be a life of lostness.

---

[47] Plato, *Apology*, p. 97.
[48] The psychological need to find meaning and purpose is discussed in greater detail in Chapter 3.

Kierkegaard's View of Socrates as Philosophical Midwife

Socrates' pathway from death-informed inquiry to an expectation of transcendent eternity was noticed and appreciated by the 19th century writer and philosopher, Søren Kierkegaard. In *Concluding Unscientific Postscript*, Kierkegaard acknowledges that there is a sense of faith in God that can emerge from a Socratic inquiry into the meaning of life.[49] As C. Stephen Evans has observed:

> Socratic faith makes possible an awareness of God that is linked to the natural moral and spiritual strivings of humans. Even if this kind of knowledge of God is less than ideal for Kierkegaard, and even though it must be sharply distinguished from the Christians' faith in Jesus, it is still real and valuable.[50]

The point of Kierkegaard's observation and appreciation of Socrates' journey toward supernaturalism is not that a teleological understanding of the cosmos (or, in today's parlance, an acceptance of the possibility of intelligent design) is equivalent to faith. Nor does Kierkegaard suggest that Socrates offers any new insights into general revelation. But Kierkegaard does highlight the fact that Socrates' notions about metaphysical realities were preceded by, and indeed were induced by, a careful philosophical introspection that took into account all of the weight, inevitability, and gloom of human mortality.

---

[49] Søren Kierkegaard, *Concluding Unscientific Postscript to Philosophical Fragments.* Trans. Howard V. Hong and Edna H. Hong (Princeton, N.J.: Princeton University Press, 1992), pp. 206-207.

[50] C. Stephen Evans. *Faith Beyond Reason: A Kierkegaardian Account* (Grand Rapids, Mich: W.B. Eerdmans Pub, 1998), p. 116.

Is it Enough to Live Well?

The Self-Enhancement View of Life

Another school of philosophy in ancient Athens was the Lyceum, founded by Aristotle (384-322 BC). Aristotle is known as one of Plato's students, and is thought to have been an early tutor for Alexander the Great during the latter's youth. In addition to his significant contributions to logic, scientific method, and metaphysics generally, Aristotle developed a theory of virtue ethics for the Western tradition. Under his approach, which was set forth in the *Rhetoric, Eudamonian Ethics,* and *Nichomachean Ethics,* the highest good and the greatest purpose in life, is to live a life of virtue.

Virtue, in turn, was defined by Aristotle as the Golden Mean between two extremes (and the extremes are usually identified as vices). For example, the virtue of courage (which is a very important trait in the Greek culture) is understood to be best represented as the midpoint between cowardice (that is, the vice of a lack of courage) and foolhardiness (that is, the vice of excessive courage).

Aristotle enjoyed a high degree of prominence among medieval philosophers and theologians (Christian, Jewish, and Islamic alike). In particular, Thomas Aquinas relied heavily on Aristotle as he articulated a Christian version of virtue ethics that emphasized human potential in terms of both pagan virtues such as courage, prudence, and temperance, and the Christian virtues of faith, hope and love.

Happiness and human flourishing is, in Aristotle's view, possible when people develop a character that is virtuous. There is, however, a certain optimism about this idea of the ethical life that seems to conflict with the realities faced by most people. Sickness, death, and evil are, in fact, very much a part of the human experience, even when life is lived virtuously. In addition not all people enjoy the same potential to flourish, as Aristotle would define flourishing, despite their character and their virtuousness: geography, history, culture, environmental conditions, family circumstances, genetics, nutrition and health, access to education, and countless other exigencies and serendipities converge to overwhelm and, to some extent, predetermine the boundaries and potentialities of each human being.

Hedonism as a Variation of the Self-Enhancement View of Life

There are a couple of ways to think about hedonism or the pursuit of pleasure as the primary purpose in life: radical hedonism and enlightened hedonism. Radical hedonism, as described by Callicles in Plato's dialogue *Gorgias*, involves maximizing the satisfaction of pleasure (494-495)[51]. In that dialogue, Callicles declares to Socrates that the highest good in life is to derive the largest possible amount of pleasure. "Unrestricted enjoyment," namely, the unrestrained satisfaction of all pleasures, is identical with good, and there is no differentiation between good pleasures and bad pleasures.[52] In fact, for Callicles, those who have the most potential for a happy life are those with the strongest appetites and the power or ability to satisfy those appetites.

Socrates himself sets forth the parameters of enlightened hedonism in the *Protagoras* (356),[53] where he describes the wisdom of weighing and measuring various types of pleasures (and various means of avoiding pain):

---

[51] Plato, and Donald J. Zeyl. *Gorgias* (Indianapolis: Hackett Pub. Co, 1987), pp. 67-69.
[52] *Ibid*, p. 68.
[53] Plato, *Protagoras and Meno* (Penguin Classics. London: Penguin Books, 2005), pp. 70-71.

You've just got to be a kind of expert at weighing things up; you've got to put together all the pleasures, and put together all the pains (placing both kinds, short- and long-term, on the scales) and then say which lot there are more of. What I mean is, if you're weighing pleasures against pleasures, then you've always got to go for the ones that are bigger and that there are more of. And if you're weighing pains against pains, you've got to go for the ones that are smaller and that there are less off. And if you're weighing up pleasures against pains, then if it turns out that the pleasures outweigh the pains (whether it's pleasures that are a long way off outweighing short-term pains, or long-term pains being outweighed by present pleasures) that's what you should do, the action that involves those pleasures; whereas if the pains outweigh the pleasures, then there's something you shouldn't do.[54]

In the same manner as the radical hedonism proposed by Callicles, the enlightenment hedonism described by Socrates is ultimately driven by a desire (and a life strategy) to maximize pleasure and minimize pain.

In the *Gorgias*, Socrates refutes Callicles' radical hedonism by pointing out that it is impractical and self-defeating. Socrates observed that the person who lives only to satisfy his or her own appetites will not exercise restraint in respecting the property or personal rights of others. They will tend to be liars, thieves and abusers because they will be wedded to the pursuit of the pleasant in lieu of the pursuit of the good. And yet if the attainment of pleasure depends at least in part on power and the ability to function effectively in society, thieves

---

[54] *Ibid*, p. 71.

and those who abuse others will not be successful in attaining power because they will not be considered trustworthy by anyone in society. Instead, they will be isolated, shunned and rendered ineffective in their efforts to enter into appetite-satisfying transactions.

Socrates' own brand of enlightened hedonism, as described in the *Protagoras*, is not without its own drawbacks. One of the problems with this evaluative approach is that not all pleasures and pains are commensurable. They cannot be measured on the same scale, or by the same standard. For example, some pleasures (such as reading a well-written and carefully researched text on the subject of existential dread) cannot reasonably be compared to others (such as eating a dish of homemade mint chocolate chip ice cream), both because they are fundamentally so different, and because they are not necessarily mutually exclusive within a given point in time.

Stoicism as a Variation of the Self-Enhancement View of Life

Emotions cause problems. They can lead us to make decisions that are irrational. More importantly, they can be very painful. If a person can suppress, master or overcome the influence of emotions, he or she might be able to live a life worth living. This was the viewpoint of those following the ancient Greek philosophical tradition of the Stoics. Within this school of thought, reason and rational thinking are paramount, and freedom from the passions, or *apatheia*, is the highest of all virtues. Self-control, and the ability to ignore or suppress pain or pleasure, were considered paramount. The expectation on the part of the Stoics was that by adopting this detachment from emotions, they would be more rational, more objective, and as a result, more effective in achieving all of their goals in life.[55]

---

[55] To the extent that the actual goals of the Stoics would have included such notions as pleasure or enjoyment, Stoicism can be viewed as a form of "long-term hedonism."

That Greek word *apatheia* is the basis for the English word "apathy." The apathy advocated by the Stoics was an intentional indifference toward passions and desires. But passions and desires are the essence of life. Indeed, as will be discussed in the next chapter, passions and emotions lie at the very center of any understanding of the "meaning of life." Passions and desires drive intentionality, and intentionality (that is, what we will, what we choose, and what motivates us) helps to reveal, if not define, who we are as individuals.[56]

Asceticism and Pragmatism as Variations of the Self-Enhancement View of Life

Asceticism, from the Greek word *askesis* (exercise, discipline), represents an ideal that is related to Stoicism. If Stoicism proper is thought of as a philosophy of short-term self-denial for the purpose of achieving a greater long-term good (physically, emotionally, economically, politically, or in some other tangible or physical way), asceticism can be thought of as denial for a different purpose. Often that different purpose is religious mysticism or some other form of transcendental achievement. Or, that purpose can simply be to make an effort to connect with the transcendental in an effort to become more whole, more functional, or more well-rounded.

The premise behind asceticism is that the natural and physical world interferes with human progress toward something higher and better. After all, the natural world is often the source of pleasures and

---

Albert Ellis, *Reason and Emotion in Psychotherapy* (Secaucus, N.J.: Citadel Press, 1962), p. 363.

[56] As Robert C. Solomon observed, "It is because we are moved, because we feel, that life has meaning. The passionate life, not the dispassionate life of pure reason, is the meaningful life. ... The passionate life of reason is the passionate life in disguise." Robert C. Solomon, *The Passions: Emotions and the Meaning of Life* (Indianapolis: Hackett Pub. Co., 1993), p. ix.

comforts that lead to self-indulgence and sin. Sometimes, as in the case of Buddhist asceticism, there is also an understanding that the human experience of suffering is caused by worldly attachments and desires. To the extent that those attachments and desires can be diminished or set aside through various rituals and disciplines, a higher, more admirable, less sinful, or more spiritual way of living (or, in the case of Buddhism, Nirvana) can be achieved.

Problems with the Self-Enhancement View of Life

It is not possible to fully comprehend and appreciate a meaning or a purpose in life after taking into account the virtue ethics theory of Aristotle without first asking about the ultimate purpose or goal of the virtues. Aristotle's teacher, Plato, advocated virtue for the sake of the city-state. That is, the ultimate goal of character development was good citizenship.

For Aristotle, the ultimate goal was a sense of happiness about life, known as *eudamonia*. By living a virtuous life, Aristotle believed, the joy of life is optimized. Self-enhancement was accomplished through disciplines that resulted in good character and virtuous habits.[57] Life, for Aristotle, was an intentional journey from ignorance to clarity and from conflict to harmony, and it would be a more successful journey to the extent that the virtues are fostered. His was an optimistic view about the potentially whole and harmonious self.

The most significant problem with the self-enhancement approach to finding purpose in life is that the virtues provide probable outcomes but not universal outcomes. If happiness, or blessedness, or comfort, becomes the goal, efforts to achieve that goal will be confounded by a

---

[57] This notion of eudamonia has enjoyed a resurgence in recent years under the name of "positive psychology." Positive psychology will be addressed in the next chapter.

lifetime of frustrations, not the least of which are sickness and death. As C.S. Lewis observed:

> In religion, as in war and everything else, comfort is the one thing you cannot get by looking for it. If you look for truth, you may find comfort in the end: if you look for comfort you will not get either comfort or truth-only soft soap and wishful thinking to begin with and, in the end, despair.[58]

In other words, even if a person develops strong, virtuous habits, the contingencies of life often overpower and overcome those habits. The honest person is sometimes done in by his or her truthfulness, when that truthfulness backfires and causes harm to the person. The courageous person can be overcome by a stronger person. Even the wisest person can be defrauded, stolen from, debilitated by illness, injured by violence, doomed by birth to a life of disability or poverty, or otherwise defeated by accidents of life. Evil too often wins out over righteousness.

To make matters worse, the vicissitudes of life (and death) loom over the battlefield of virtues and vices. The Aristotelian project of providing a conception of happiness derived from the attainment of virtues is, at the individual level, an inevitable failure. Virtues ensure nothing more than probabilities: one person's pursuit of the Golden Mean may allow him or her to flourish more than another person who, for example, pursues immediate pleasures and comforts without regard to the development of good habits. In the end, however, the guaranteed vicissitudes of sickness, death, and the turmoils of life will trump and

---

[58] C. S. Lewis, *Mere Christianity: A Revised and Amplified Edition, with a New Introduction, of the Three Books, Broadcast Talks, Christian Behaviour, and Beyond Personality* (San Francisco: HarperSanFrancisco, 2001), p. 32.

inevitably overcome any improvements in life that might be augmented as a result of virtuous living. And in the end, even if a person's wisdom and virtue would seem to have forestalled death by a day, a week, a year, or more, death always wins. A life lived virtuously makes for a better eulogy, but the eulogy is nevertheless spoken at a funeral.

Thomas Aquinas (1225 - 1274) built on the Aristotelian model by blending in the theological virtues of faith, hope and charity. For Aquinas, the ultimate goal of the virtues was a sort of Christianized good person. This was still a form of self-enhancement, but it was self-enhancement for the sake of living a life that was consistent with the Bible and with church doctrines. Aquinas, like Aristotle, understood the human structure as being a potentially harmonious combination of body and soul, and that the optimized human life involved the enhancement and fostering of both by the development of the virtues.

Blaise Pascal (1623-1662) was one of the first thinkers to question the Thomist notion of a body-and-soul in harmony. He recognized an inherent dissonance between the two, one that was not resolved by fully acceding to either the body (as in the case of, for example, hedonism) or the soul (as in the case of, for example, asceticism). The human being is a truth-seeker who is compelled to wrestle with the seemingly disparate requirements of both body and soul:

> Shall he say then, on the contrary, that he certainly possesses truth-he who, when pressed ever so little, can show no title to it, and is forced to let go his hold? What a chimera then is man! What a novelty! What a monster, what a chaos, what a contradiction, what a prodigy! Judge of all things, imbecile worm of the earth; depository of truth, a sink of uncertainty and error; the pride and refuse of the universe! Who will

unravel the tangle? Nature confounds the skeptics, and
reason can diffuse the dogmatists.[59]

Pascal did not assign the designations "despair" or "dread" to this
dissonance between body and soul, but he did recognize the frustration
engendered by this conflict. He saw the difficulty of attempting to live
within the tension and to be fully alive to it.

However it is articulated or constructed, the self-enhancement view
of life is motivated and animated by hope, but it is a false hope. This is
because it is a hope that depends upon the self. Only if the individual is
successful in developing virtues, optimizing pleasures, or constructing
a safe and pain-free environment, can the self-enhancement view begin
to deliver on its promises. As already noted, for most people at most
times in most places around the world, it does not matter, and it
will not matter, how disciplined or effective they are in developing
skills and habits that would enhance their lives. Life does not seem to
accommodate and reward their efforts. Irrespective of such efforts, it
is as if the ground is cursed (Genesis 3:17).

There is even a life cycle of hope-shattering that is not uncommon
in North American culture. Children are often told "you can do
anything you want to in life," and in many cases are encouraged to
"dream big" about their expectations of life. In addition, throughout
their school years, children are often encouraged to foster their own
self-esteem, and are praised for their accomplishments, large and small.
By the time they graduate from high school, they have been saturated
with a sense of optimism and expectation.

Eventually, however, the realities of life catch up with most young
adults. They find themselves lowering their expectations, often to the
point where they find themselves struggling to maintain a modicum

---

[59] Blaise Pascal, and W. F. Trotter. *Pensées* (Mineola, N.Y.: Dover Publications,
2003), p. 121.

of a comfortable lifestyle. Meanwhile, the drudgery of mundane jobs and everyday responsibilities serve to further erode the big dreams they were encouraged to foster in their youth. The pursuit of a life of functionality, not self-optimization, captures the center of their attention. This can be depressing. As Gabriel Marcel (1889-1973) notes:

> Life in a world centered on function is liable to despair because in reality the world is *empty*, it rings hollow; and if it resists the temptation, it is only to the extent that they are come into play from within it and in its favor certain hidden forces which are beyond its power to conceive or to recognize.[60]

Worse, even if the individual is successful in the implementation of the self-enhancement view of life, hope is too often sabotaged by ambition or pride, or both. Ambition, because the drive for self-enhancement is seldom sated. There is always another mountain to climb, or another barrier to overcome. Pride, because there is a natural tendency to attribute success (however measured) to one's own skills and abilities. As Marcel explained this phenomenon:

> I believe it must be answered that, speaking metaphysically, *the only genuine hope is hope in what does not depend on ourselves*, hope springing from humility and not from pride... as far as pride, it consists in drawing one's strength solely from oneself. The proud man is cut off from a certain form of communion with

---

[60] Gabriel Marcel, *The Philosophy of Existentialism* (New York: Citadel Press, 2002), p. 32.

his fellow men, which pride, acting as a principle of destruction, tends to break down.[61]

Living in Kierkegaard's Basement

A life lived hedonistically, stoically, or pragmatically hardly fares better (or worse) than a life lived virtuously. Kierkegaard lumps all of these various approaches to life into a notion of living aesthetically. That is, for Kierkegaard, a life lived aesthetically is a life lived in pursuit of self-fulfillment or self-enhancement, in opposition to a life lived in submission to an external deity, an external universal set of laws, or some other external or objective standard. Kierkegaard considers this approach to life, with its emphasis on various levels and types of self-gratification, pleasure, and worldly pursuits as a lower sphere of existence.

Kierkegaard uses the metaphor of a house to describe what he understood to be the various phases or spheres of existence:

> Imagine a house with a basement, first floor, and second-floor planned so that there is or is supposed to be a social distinction between the occupants according to floor. Now, if what it means to be a human being is compared with such a house, then all too regrettably this sad and ludicrous truth about the majority of people is that in their own house they prefer to live in the basement.[62]

---

[61] *Ibid*, p. 12.
[62] Kierkegaard, Søren, Howard V. Hong, and Edna H. Hong. *The Sickness unto Death: a Christian Psychological Exposition for Upbuilding and Awakening* (Princeton, N.J.: Princeton University Press, 1980), pp. 43-44.

By living in the basement, Kierkegaard is referring to the aesthetic sphere, with its focus on self-enhancement. He understood that if we live within the framework of aesthetic existence, we are restlessly anxious. We seek to be enchanted and enthralled by persons, places and things, and we look to those persons, places and things as our Messiah. The pursuit of personal relationships, the arts, and any other human aspirations or endeavors, are ultimately targeted toward self enhancement (which Kierkegaard understands to be self-love).

This is a hermeneutical cycle that leaves us in the basement unless and until we seek something external to ourselves for its own sake. So long as we are living for the moment, we are searching for infinite variety and enhancement. It is only when we realize that we have lost our self to the chase for that which yet intrigues us, and we despair of such loss of self, that we can recover hope: hope to escape the hermeneutical circle.

For Kierkegaard, then, being trapped in this hermeneutical cycle was reason for despair. As it happens, though, not everyone adopts, pursues or maintains a sufficient level of self-consciousness so as to be aware of such lostness and despair. For some people, the angst is little more than a slight anxiousness about making decisions in pursuit of this or that pleasure or self-enhancement. For others, the paradox of pursuing various goals, but never attaining true happiness or self-actualization even if some of those goals are reached, leads to full-fledged philosophical melancholy. In other words, there is an interdependence between the intensity of self-consciousness and the likelihood that a person is aware of her or his entrapment in the hermeneutical circle:

> Every human being is a psychical-physical synthesis intended to be spirit; this is the building, but he prefers to live in the basement, that is, in sensate

categories. Moreover, he not only prefers to live in the basement-no, he loves it so much that he is indignant if anyone suggests that he move to the superb upper floor that stands vacant and at his disposal, for he is, after all, living in his own house.[63]

Is it Enough to Live Rightly?

The Ethical-Duty View of Life

Both the self-enhancement and the self-verification views of life are, by definition, self-centered and self-oriented. As described above, they are also largely empty and are not reliably self-satisfying, especially in the face of the vicissitudes of life.

A third philosophical approach to finding or establishing meaning or purpose in life is the ethical-duty approach. This is not the only "ethical" approach to life: many of the virtues advocated in the self-enhancement view of life are other-oriented and are decidedly ethical in nature. Similarly, the virtue of authenticity (or, more precisely, authentic-ness), as promoted in the self-verification approach to life, is itself considered to be the most genuine approach to living.[64]

The emphasis of the ethical-duty view, however, is slightly different. It points toward the following of ethical norms and rules for their own sake, rather than for the sake of optimizing or authenticating one's life. For example, if the Golden Rule is interpreted from a self-enhancement perspective, it can be understood to read, "Do unto others as you would have them do unto you, because in the end that works best for you." But if that same Golden Rule is interpreted from an ethical-duty perspective, it can be understood to read "Do unto others as you would

---

[63] *Ibid.*

[64] The self-verification approach to life is considered below.

have them do onto you because that is a rule that you ought to live by for its own sake."

Of course, the words "for its own sake" could be changed to something else. If the Golden Rule is understood within a religious context, the words "for its own sake" can be changed to "for God's sake" or, in the case of some religions, for the sake of an enhanced karma, or Nirvana, or Paradise, or some sort of future existence in another life. Religion, and in particular many forms and expressions of religion, often represents an effort to turn toward asceticism. Asceticism is sometimes understood in a religious context as an effort to discipline or purify one's soul from the lower passions in an effort to become more God-like or more God-pleasing.[65] The rituals and activities that accompany this effort, such as self-deprivation, fasting, vigils, and prolonged prayer and meditation, have the purpose (or the effect) of dulling the senses[66]. In any event, most religions take on the project of drawing the individual away from self-centered tendencies and toward something else. As part of that process, ethical duties and rules are often prescribed.

The words "for its own sake" could also be changed to "for the sake of society." This is the essential claim of the Enlightenment philosophers of ethics. Utilitarians, such as John Stuart Mill (1806-1873), claimed that individuals ought to take into account how a person's actions would contribute to the greatest amount of happiness for the largest number of people in society, and adjust their behavior

---

[65] F. L. Cross, *The Oxford Dictionary of the Christian Church* (London: Oxford University Press, 1966), p. 93.

[66] *Ibid.* Max Weber understood asceticism, and especially Puritan asceticism, as effort to zealously turn against "one thing in particular: *the uninhibited enjoyment of life* and of the pleasures it has to offer." Max Weber, Peter Baehr, and Gordon C. Wells, *The Protestant Ethic and the "Spirit" of Capitalism and Other Writings* (New York: Penguin Books, 2002), pp. 112-113. His italics.

accordingly. The "greatest happiness of the greatest number" was Mill's rallying cry.[67]

Similarly, proponents of social contract theory claimed that individual actions should be measured against the requirements of society in general, as articulated through laws, regulations, and social norms. In the end, the most ethical person is the person whose self-interests, however derived or understood, are authenticated or validated only so long as they are consistent with a larger view of the well-being of society in general. If there is a conflict between self-interest and the interest of society, society ought to win out over the individual.

Immanuel Kant might have preferred changing the expression "for its own sake," to, "for the sake of practical reason." Kant crafted an ethical regime that largely resembles basic Judeo-Christian ethics, but that purportedly relies on reason alone (without reference to sacred text, God or religion). For Kant, morality was the object of pure practical reason, and moral behavior is the result of a proper adoption and application of moral maxims that conform to universal moral principles.[68]

Kierkegaard uses the idea of marrying and raising a family as an example of how a person might move from the aesthetic (self-enhancement) view of life, to the ethical view. By taking on familial responsibilities, the individual learns to live and love within an ethical network of concentric circles. The father, for example, learns to love his wife and children. The family, in turn, develops a mutual interdependence among its members, as well as in regard to the larger concentric circle of friends and neighbors, and then the community, the

---

[67] *See* John Stuart Mill, quoting Jeremy Bentham, "Cooperation: Intended Speech, 1825" in John Stuart Mill and John M. Robson. *Journals and Debating Speeches* (Toronto: University of Toronto Press, 1988), p. 309.

[68] Immanuel Kant, *Critique of Practical Reason* (New York: Liberal Arts Press, 1956), p. 65.

nation, the earth, etc. Despite this outward-looking ethical engagement, the ethical rules and norms are never absolutized. That is, the ethical life always involves a certain amount of anxiety in regard to decision-making, even when the framework for the required decisions is not limited to self-enhancement.

Problems with the Ethical-Duty View of Life

The ethical-duty approach to life, then, is not self-centered, even though most people are largely self-centered (much, if not most, of the time). Yet, it tends to result in failure and frustration for those who attempt to adopt it. To the extent that the ethical life is not motivated by an effort to be honored, respected or otherwise well thought of (any or all of which would move the agent out of the ethical life and into the self-enhancement approach to life), the orientation toward duty for its own sake is largely unpleasant, tiresome, boring, and unattractive. To the extent that the ethical life is adopted in order to please God, it tends to result in a form of legalism that, in turn, reduces God to a taskmaster who extracts selflessness as a price for acceptance. The very possibility that the ethical life might somehow be influenced by, informed by, dictated by, or otherwise affected by God, is itself a problem in the Western philosophical tradition. The original house that Kierkegaard built had a second floor, and that second floor was occupied by God. Kierkegaard did not believe that living an ethical life (on the first floor) provided access to God. Instead, he accepted the orthodox Protestant understanding that a relationship with God requires faith, and in particular, a radical faith premised solely on the work of Jesus Christ rather than on the work of the individual believer. Nevertheless, he understood the principle that the only truly ethical life is one that is lived in conformity with God's law and God's holiness as articulated in the traditional Judeo-Christian scriptures.

Of course, not everyone accepts the premise that an ethical life is one that is conformed to Judeo-Christian biblical morality. Much of the Enlightenment project involved an effort to articulate ethics without any reference to, or dependence on, the Judeo-Christian tradition. That effort was a failure in two ways: first, the Enlightenment project was unable to craft a compelling, persuasive ethical regime that would captivate the human heart. Instead, the utilitarianism of John Stuart Mill and the deontological ethics of Immanuel Kant proved to be dry, soulless, unpersuasive and hardly relevant to most individuals in the normal course of their everyday lives. As Steven D. Smith framed it, "many people find that utilitarianism simply does not adequately grasp or express their deeper normative commitments."[69]

Second, the Enlightenment project was also a failure because it did not successfully create ethical norms *ab initio* and *ex nihilo*. In other words, ethical norms proposed by Enlightenment ethicists bore a striking resemblance to those of the Ten Commandments. The Judeo-Christian heritage had not been avoided.

In the decades and centuries following the 18th century Enlightenment project, greater efforts were expended in the development of a rationalized ability to ignore the God of the second floor, or to deny the existence of God (and the second floor) entirely. This effort continues today and is carried forth most prominently by a group known as the New Atheists. Such authors as Sam Harris, Daniel C. Dennett, Richard Dawkins, and Christopher Hitchens proffer a hard-line, militant narrative that considers a belief in God to be not only irrational, but pathological and dangerous to society. They generally insist that there can be such a thing as ethics, but their ideas about ethics are relativistic and do not map to or rely upon any objective, universal ethical principles. They would blow up, tear down or otherwise destroy the second floor of Kierkegaard's house.

---

[69] Steven D. Smith, *The Disenchantment of Secular Discourse* (Cambridge, Mass: Harvard University Press, 2010), p. 25.

And so a second problem of living on the second floor is that unless ethical rules are warranted by some external higher authority, they have no meaning or credibility. They amount to little more than social preferences, and their enforcement depends upon positive law and power rather than any type of warranted moral suasion. Despite such lack of warrant, life on the first floor of a one-story building seems to be popular enough. So much so, that Nietzsche's aphorism that "God is dead" was as much an observation of how society was functioning (that is, with little more than nominal gestures in the direction of religion and Judeo-Christian orthodoxy and traditions), as it was a declaration of real atheism.

Living on the First Floor of Kierkegaard's House

To the extent that the ethical, first-floor life is understood to have been founded upon God's law, there is a need to revisit that law on a regular basis. If the Mosaic law, especially as expounded upon by Jesus in the Sermon on the Mount, is held out to be the standard, failure is inevitable. This is the "moral of the story" of much of the Bible, including all of the Old Testament, and including much of what Jesus had to say during his lifetime on earth. Paul summarizes this moral of the story in his letter to the Romans and elsewhere in the New Testament.

On the other hand, to the extent that an effort is made to live an ethical life without reference to God's law, there is no external standard by which to measure the success or failure of the ethical life. Instead, the individual must reflect inward and determine based on his or her "gut" or other similar subjective resources, which can prove unreliable. Many heinous crimes have been committed by those who believed they were doing the right thing.

Alternatively, self-assessment of first-floor living can be achieved by looking to others. If a person's "ethical" behavior seems to be appreciated, accepted, admired, and honored by those in his or her circle of friends and family, some sense of validation can result. However, entire families, communities, villages, countries and cultures have from time to time adopted mores (such as infanticide, sati, genocide, slavery, sexual promiscuity, debasement of women, etc.) that other cultures and societies would deem morally wrong. At best, this effort to measure ethical behavior by reference to others within the community mimics the honor-seeking approach to self-enhancement living in the basement of Kierkegaard's house. At worst, it highlights the lack of any foundation for the ethical life.

And so, as Kierkegaard pointed out, the only intellectually honest response to first-floor living is despair. There is an exasperation that results from an attempt to live a godly life, only to discover that God's standards are beyond reach. And there is the horror of discovering that any attempt to live an ethical life without reference to God's law (or some similar external set of universal principles) is fraudulent: it proves to be subjective, amoral, and entirely without foundation or basis.

The discovery of failure and despair within the first floor of Kierkegaard's house is unremitting and repetitive. Every time the first-floor dweller attempts to measure his or her progress, failure and hopelessness reappear and reassert themselves. When undergoing this assessment, the individual is forced to acknowledge that he or she has failed to truly live the prescribed ethical life flawlessly, and yet the individual must choose whether or not to continue in his or her effort to live the ethical life. Kierkegaard considers this choosing and re-choosing of the ethical life to be itself a choice of despair. As he has Judge Wilhelm explaining:

> Anyone who chooses himself ethically has himself as a
> task . . . The person who lives ethically has seen himself,

knows himself, permeates his whole concretion with his consciousness . . . The ethical individual knows himself, but this knowledge is not mere contemplation . . . it is a reflection on himself, which is itself an action, and that is why I have been careful to use the expression 'to choose oneself' instead of 'to know oneself'" Although inward reflection reveals one's condition of despair, which is itself a choice, the ethical life requires more than introspection and contemplation. It requires a reflection that responds through the act of choice and for the purpose of living an authentic, determined, and inevitably ethical life.[70]

Even though the ethical life involves despair, it is a different kind of despair from that experienced as part of the self-enhancement life. It is first-floor despair, rather than basement despair. It is despair that is derived from the frustration at making limited, finite decisions and reductive efforts within a framework of universal principles (or lack of universal principles) and, along the way, rediscovering corresponding infinite demands.

Is it Enough to Be Authentic?

The Self-Verification View of Life

If Aristotle's admonition can be summarized as "Be the best that you are," it comes close to Nietzsche's admonition "Become what you are." More precisely, in the *Gay Science*, Nietzsche answers the question "What does your conscience say?" with the exhortation that "You

---

[70] Søren Kierkegaard and Alastair Hannay. *Either/or: A Fragment of Life* (London, England: Penguin Books, 1992), p. 549.

shall become the person you are."[71] In other words, authenticate your existence.

This notion of authenticity was popularized by Jean-Paul Sartre (1905-1980), for whom the concept consists in "having a true and lucid consciousness of the situation, in assuming the responsibilities and risks it involves, in accepting it in pride or humiliation, sometimes in horror and hate."[72] To be authentic, for Sartre, means, first of all, to deny any presuppositions about human nature and accept the notions that "Man is nothing else but that which he makes of himself"[73] and, by extension, "nothing else but what he purposes, he exists only in so far as he realizes himself, he is therefore nothing else but the sum of his actions, nothing else but what his life is."[74] Sartre's idea of authenticity was not the self-as-self, but rather, the self as achievement.

Despite his emphasis on the self-as-subject, Sartre attempted to avoid the radical individualism that had earlier been associated with René Descartes (1596-1650). He did this by crafting a strong view of inter-subjectivity that recognized others (or specifically, "the other") as subject as well. As he explained this notion:

> The other is indispensable to my existence and equally so to any knowledge I can have of myself. Under these conditions, the ultimate discovery of myself is at the same time the revelation of the other as a freedom

---

[71] Friedrich Wilhelm Nietzsche, and Walter Arnold Kaufmann. *The Gay Science; With a Prelude in Rhymes and an Appendix of Songs* (New York: Vintage Books, 1974), p. 219.

[72] Jean-Paul Sartre and George Joseph Becker. *Anti-Semite and Jew* (New York: Schocken Books, 1965), p. 90.

[73] Jean-Paul Sartre, "Existentialism is a Humanism," in Walter Kaufman, editor. *Existentialism from Dostoevsky to Sartre* (New York: World Publishing, 1965), p. 291.

[74] *Ibid*, p. 300.

which confronts mine, and which cannot think or will without doing so either for or against me.[75]

Sartre developed a corresponding existentialist concept of *mauvaise foi,* or bad faith, in terms of inauthenticity.[76] His notion of bad faith involved any effort to define oneself, because to do so is to reduce oneself to the object of such definition. This self-consciousness is a turning inward, but for Sartre such a turn inward actually reveals nothing (or, more specifically, nothingness). There is no inherent human nature that can serve as a reference point for morality or meaning, and, accordingly, true authenticity is, for Sartre, understood in terms of the outgoing expression of our consciousness prior to any self-reflection. We are that which we choose and do throughout our life, and so when we do not choose for ourselves, our inaction is inherently in bad faith.

For Kierkegaard, bad faith not only involved inaction, but it involved being subsumed into the culture to the point of losing one's identity and one's self in the crowd. In a sense, Kierkegaard was the first to complain about "political correctness," because, for him, the turn toward the crowd was inevitably a turn away from eternal truth. Cultural peer pressure tears away from individual authenticity:

> The immorality of our age is perhaps not lost in pleasure and sensuality, but rather a pantheistic, debauched contempt for individual human beings. In the midst of the jubilation over our age and the 19th century there sounds a secret contempt for being a human being-in the midst of the importance of the generation there is a despair over being a human being. Everything,

---

[75] *Ibid*, p. 303.

[76] Jean-Paul Sartre, *Being and Nothingness; An Essay on Phenomenological Ontology* (New York: Philosophical Library, 1956), pp. 86-88.

everything must be together; people want to delude themselves world-historically in the totality; no one wants to be an individual existing human being.[77]

Problems with the Self-Verification View of Life

To say that I am that which I do, reduces me to my will and my actions. There is no sin (or, in Socratic terms, there is no *akrasia*), because there is no standard except that of the genuineness. If, for example, I am a genuine murderer or rapist, that is who I am. I am an authentic murderer or rapist, and any attempt to thwart my acting out of my choices is oppressive. Such an attempt objectifies me and forces me to either make excuses for what I have done, or to accept a standard of behavior other than my own authentic expression of myself.

The problem, then, with the self authentication approach is that because the self-referential standard is radically subjective, it is no standard at all. The atheist existentialists such as Sartre and Camus saw authenticity as the only remaining option for meaning in life once all of the other options, including God, were eliminated. Happiness, or the well-lived life, could not be socially constructed. It had to come from within.

For many people, however, authenticity-seeking is a dead-end. It results in loneliness because it calls upon the individual to turn inward and to derive meaning by observing one's self. If the human being is nothing but a project, what if the project is a failure? Worse, what if there is no identifiable project? This results in emptiness, because we are embedded in the world, and we seem to require meaning that corresponds to and coheres with our empirical experiences. And it results in narcissism, which is unsatisfying, if not depressing.

---

[77] Søren Kierkegaard, Howard V. Hong, and Edna H. Hong. *The Point of View* (Princeton, N.J.: Princeton University Press, 1998), p. 355.

If being starts with the subjective, it has no basis, and therefore it has no reason for being. As Marcel observed, "the need of being can deny itself."[78] What if a person seems to himself or herself to be wholly inadequate at self-authentication? This is the dilemma articulated by Marcel:

> My life, and by reflection all life, may appear to me as forever inadequate to something which I carry within me, which in a sense I am, but which reality rejects and excludes. Despair is possible in any form, at any moment and to any degree, and this betrayal may seem to be counseled, if not forced upon us, by the very structure of the world we live in. The deadly aspect of this world may, from a given standpoint, be regarded as a ceaseless indictment to denial and to suicide. It could be said in this sense that the fact that suicide is always possible is the essential starting point of any genuine metaphysical thought.[79]

This ceaseless indictment to denial and to suicide requires a continual re-visitation and re-invention of self, resulting in an eternal state of *not-yet-being* and despair.

Is there Nothing to Seek?

The Post-Modern View of Life

What if there is nothing "out there"? What if the world, and all reality, is chaos? What if it is impossible to gain a sure understanding of truth itself? What if there is no real basis for arriving at any conclusions

---

[78] Marcel, *Existentialism*, p. 26.
[79] *Ibid.*

about truth or God, morality, or anything metaphysical? Nihilism is the view that values and morality and even knowledge cannot be justified. The only absolute truth is that all is nothing.

Nihilism is often premised upon a radical form of skepticism, that is, a deep suspicion about whether anything can be truly known. As *Gorgias* described this phenomenon:

> Nothing exists. And if anything did exist, it would be unknowable. And if anything were knowable, it would be incommunicable.[80]

By definition, nihilism denies that there can be truth about meaning or purpose in life.

Nihilism is the basis for, or the natural outcome of, relativism. In the words of one author, nihilism "embraces" relativism.[81] For another, nihilism and relativism "join hands."[82] However it is articulated, relativism focuses on the understandings, mores, and practices of a particular society or group at a certain point in time. There is no objective or external anchor, and even truth itself is understood to be a grasp of reality that will likely be adjusted and changed over time.

Post-modernism, in turn, is a generalized malaise and mood of vagueness that takes into account the failures of rationalism and modernism. While there are many definitions and genres of "post-modernism," the term is used here to suggest a response to, and a break from, confidence in the reliance upon the human rationalism

---

[80] Kathleen Freeman and Hermann Diels. *Ancilla to The Pre-Socratic Philosophers: A Complete Translation of the Fragments in Diels Fragmente Der Vorsokratiker.* (Oxford: Basil Blackwell, 1956), pp. 128-129.

[81] Mark Holmes, "A Response to Bowers, Howard, Stanley and Soltis," *American Journal of Education*, 94, no. 4 (Aug., 1986), p. 540.

[82] Margaret S. Archer, "Resisting the Revival of Relativism," *International Sociology*, 2, no. 3 (Sept., 1987), p. 235.

that came into being with the Renaissance and was idolized, if not worshiped, as part of the Enlightenment.[83] This understanding of post-modernism is inspired by Nietzche and, to some extent, Heidegger, and is largely a perspective of gloom, an awareness of the demise of the self as "subject," and a skepticism both about truth itself, as well as about the possibility of representing truth.

There is an inherent sense of emptiness that seems to accompany this nihilistic view of life. If there is nothing "out there," if material-natural-empirical reality is the only reality, there is an accompanying disenchantment with life. And there is despair because a life lived within this paradigm involves taking and accepting unenchanted relativisms as if they were absolute and enchanted. Kierkegaard, through the voice of Johannes di Silentio, expresses this disenchantment well:

> If a human being did not have an eternal consciousness, if underlying everything there were only a wild, fermenting power that writhing in dark passions produced everything, be it significant or insignificant, if a vast never appeased emptiness hid beneath everything, what would life be then but despair? If such were the situation, if there were no sacred bond that knit humankind together, if one generation emerged after another like forest foliage, if one generation succeeded another like the singing of birds in the forest, if a generation passed through the world as a ship through the sea, as wind through the desert, an unthinking and unproductive performance, if an eternal oblivion,

---

[83] This is consistent with Lyotard's articulation of a post-modern mood or state of mind that is generally pessimistic, skeptical and nihilistic. *See* Jean-François Lyotard, *The Postmodern Condition: A Report on Knowledge* (Minneapolis: University of Minnesota Press, 1984).

perpetually hungry, lurked for its prey and there were
no power strong enough to wrench that away from it –
how empty and devoid of consolation life would be![84]

The project of overcoming philosophical despair through philosophy has been well tried and tested. It is a failure. It failed for Jacques Maritain and Raïssa Oumansoff, who were rescued from their suicide pact by faith rather than by philosophy. Philosophy, it turns out, is much better at pointing toward the darkness, than at providing illumination and hope.

Philosophical discussions about meaning in life get bogged down in the quicksand of nominalism and the critique of language itself. Efforts to sort out and differentiate the physical from the metaphysical become lost in a fog of deeper questions about reality itself. Models for articulating and depicting what it means to live a good life show much promise, and are largely ignored in face of the temptations and vicissitudes of life. The ideal "good person" can be readily described in terms of honor, admirability, love, respectability, credibility, and so forth but altruism is easily and readily corrupted by human desires for significance, power, wealth or control. Nietzsche's view, that human life is largely driven by a will to power, seems to trump Aristotle's view that human life is driven by the desire for *eudamonia*.

The Death of Philosophy

"Philosophy is dead." This is a statement that was made at least as early as 1956 by Peter Laslett[85] and as recently as September 2010

---

[84] Søren Kierkegaard, Howard V. Hong, and Edna H. Hong, *Fear and Trembling; Repetition* (Princeton, N.J.: Princeton University Press, 1983), p. 15.
[85] Peter Laslett, *Philosophy, Politics and Society; A Collection* (Oxford: Blackwell, 1956), p. vii ("For the moment, anyway, philosophy is dead.").

by Stephen Hawking.[86] In other words, philosophy has nothing to say anymore. To the extent that philosophy has provided a methodology, or a way of thinking about and asking about life, philosophy is truly dead if philosophy no longer has anything to offer about these thoughts in these questions. And to the extent that philosophy involves the seeking of answers to larger questions, philosophy is dead if those answers are no longer considered to be accessible, meaningful, or worth seeking.

There are three different, but related, ways to think about the death of philosophy. First, the death of philosophy can simply be another way of saying that philosophy tends to lead to despair. This has already been described above. The self-enhancement view of life tends to result in the paradox of hedonism, that is, despair at the discovery that most varieties of self-enhancement lead to the same place: a focus on oneself that ultimately tends to be uninspiring, uninteresting, and pointless. Similarly, the self-verification and the ethical-rule approaches to life often lead to a similar process of intellectual and spiritual exhaustion. Philosophy has proven adept at crafting the great questions of life; it has proven inept at providing robust answers that make the ideal real, and that ensure enduring metaphysical meaningfulness. It is as if the project of philosophical pursuit offers little more than a vaporous vanity (Ecclesiastes 1:2).

The more recent Hawking-style pronouncement of the death of philosophy, however, has a somewhat different basis. This second

---

[86] Stephen W. Hawking and Leonard Mlodinow. *The Grand Design* (New York: Bantam Books, 2010), p. 5 ("Philosophy is dead. It has not kept up with modern developments in science, particularly physics. Scientists have become the bearers of the torch of discovery in our quest for knowledge."). It should also be noted that this reductive notion that philosophy is dead is often associated with Richard Rorty, whose work, *Philosophy and the Mirror of Nature* (Princeton: Princeton University Press, 1979) includes Rorty's characterization of philosophy as merely hoping to "underwrite or debunk claims to knowledge made by science, morality, art or religion" (p. 3).

view of the death of philosophy is, in a sense, the completion of the Enlightenment project of human rationalism. That project was characterized by a bifurcation and partitioning of the metaphysical from the physical, the ideal from the tangible, and beliefs from knowledge. This emphasis on, and preference for, naturalistic scientism has served to compartmentalize faith as belief in something unreal, and to treat values as being little more than emotivist preferences that do not derive from, or add to, the body of scientific and empirically verified knowledge. To the extent that philosophy tends to drift in the direction of the metaphysical and the ideal, philosophy is effectively dead because the ideal and the metaphysical are irrelevant specters of non-knowledge. Philosophy may as well be dead, if it has nothing more to say about scientific discovery than, say, literature or most of the other humanities.

There is a third understanding of the death of philosophy that is even more radical than that offered by secular scientism. This third view considers the sciences (hard and soft, physical and social) to have no more credibility than the humanities. This post-modern view is skeptical of all knowledge, irrespective of its content or the manner in which it is derived. Instead, all science, all philosophy, all literature, and all efforts to communicate knowledge are hampered by the linguistic agenda of the proponents of these would-be disciplines. To the extent that philosophy and, in particular, analytical philosophy, would represent an attempt to somehow rescue knowledge from the corruption of language and power-seeking impulses of the speakers of language, philosophy is dead because it cannot be relied upon to achieve such a rescue. Most philosophers, as the saying goes, are "dead white males," and philosophy cannot be expected to rise above its heritage and rescue the language.

Conclusion: Despair and Dread

Despair

The term "despair" has been used thus far to describe a possible and reasonable (if not inevitable) consequence of philosophical inquiry. The single word "despair" can, of course, mean different things in different settings, as can the expression "philosophical despair." As used here, despair refers to two specific phenomena: cognitive hopelessness and the elusiveness of infinitude.

Cognitive hopelessness is the recognition that the mind cannot resolve the emotional and spiritual quest for fulfillment. As described above in regard to the various ways in which purpose and meaning are sought through philosophical resources and methodologies, we cannot reliably reason our way to *eudaimonia,* or happiness, or significance or any other state of ultimate contentment. Satisfaction of physical and biological appetites, needs, and urges does not fully satisfy, and intellectual efforts to satisfy what ultimately seem to be emotional and spiritual yearnings for meaning and purpose too often prove unfruitful.

Related to cognitive hopelessness is the notion of the elusiveness of infinitude. There is an impulse within the human heart to seek the transcendent, and to touch that which is beyond one's grasp. The young child learns to count, and soon realizes that one plus one is the beginning of a sequence of numbers that never ends; one plus one plus one ultimately leads to the outer darkness of mathematical infinity. We can imagine infinity, and timelessness, and what might lie beyond the outer regions of the universe, but we cannot touch them. Instead, we are reminded of our own physical limitations. We are reminded of death. As Søren Kierkegaard observed, this reminder points us to a specific category of philosophical tension that is, itself, a form of despair:

> Consequently, every human existence which has supposedly become, or simply wants to be, infinite-yes, any instance in which a human existence has become or simply wants to be infinite-is despair. For the self is a synthesis in which the finite is the confining factor, the infinite the expanding factor.[87]

It is as if eternity has been embedded within the heart of the mortal human being (Ecclesiastes 3:11), much to his or her frustration and dismay.

Dread

If despair is presumed to be a mostly intellectual acknowledgment of the exhaustion of hope, dread can be described as a somewhat more emotional and psychological awakening in response to, among other things, despair. Dread, especially as used by Kierkegaard, refers to an anxiety about the unknown. If despair is a recognition that hopes and expectations have been effectively erased, dread is a repulsion in response to the resulting vacuum. It is a fearfulness in regard to the unknown, as opposed to fear in response to a recognized or known threat.

This sense of dread as a generalized anxiety about the unknown is famously captured by Shakespeare in the familiar *Hamlet* soliloquy that begins with the question, "To be, or not to be?"[88] There, it is suggested that the "dread of something after death" is more troubling than death itself, so much so that the "undiscover'd country from whose bourn,

---

[87] Søren Kierkegaard and Alastair Hannay, *The Sickness Unto Death: A Christian Psychological Exposition for Edification and Awakening* (London, England: Penguin Books, 1989), p. 80.

[88] William Shakespeare, "Hamlet," *The Complete Works of William Shakespeare* (New York: World Syndicate, 1970), p. 688.

No traveller returns, puzzles the will" and ultimately "makes cowards of us all."[89]

Dread, then, is the refusal to dwell comfortably within the despair proffered by philosophy. In some ways, dread is the willful negation of nihilism. It is the stubborn reawakening of the human yearning for hope despite apparent hopelessness. It is the persistent spark of insistence that being-in-nothingness is either a lie, or must necessarily be a temporary but erroneous understanding of the reality of human existence. If philosophy is indeed dead, dread represents the unwillingness to arrive at the final stage of grief, that is, acceptance.

---

[89] *Ibid.*

3

DREAD AND THE PSYCHOLOGICAL
SEARCH FOR MEANING

Nothing happens while you live. The scenery changes,
people come and go out, that's all. There are no beginning.
Days are tacked onto days.

Jean-Paul Sartre[90]

A Universal Human Quest

The story is told about the philosopher Arthur Schopenhauer (1788-
1860), who habitually strolled through a Berlin park in the early hours
of the morning in wrinkled clothing and sockless feet. One morning,
while seated on a park bench, Schopenhauer was sternly questioned by
a conscientious police officer: "Who are you?" In true philosophical
form, Schopenhauer answered, "I wish to God I knew."

---

[90] Jean-Paul Sartre, *Nausea*, trans. Lloyd Alexander (New York: New Directions,
1964), p. 38.

The desire to find and grasp meaning in life reflected in Schopenhauer's quip is not limited to philosophers. Pope John Paul II once observed that "a cursory glance at ancient history shows clearly how in different parts of the world, with their different cultures, there arise at the same time the fundamental questions which pervade human life: Who am I? Where have I come from and where am I going?"[91] For humans to ask these kinds of questions is a universal urge and a universal quest. It signifies an innate sense of alienation, a sense of lostness of personal identity, and a desire to identify with something larger than one's self. It is not only a philosophical concept, but a psychological one as well.

Viktor Frankl and Meaning-Based Psychotherapy

In 1940, Viktor E. Frankl (1905-1997), a young psychiatrist who had studied Schopenhauer and who had engaged in a rather intense correspondence with Sigmund Freud, brought the questions, "Who am I and why am I here?" into the domain of psychotherapy. Early in his career, Frankl began to develop his own brand of analysis called *logotherapy*, based on a definition of the Greek word *logos* as "meaning." Logotherapy was founded on the notion that within the human experience is an innate need to find meaning and purpose in life[92]. Frankl came to believe that dealing with that human need for meaning was a prerequisite to the achievement of any sense of contentment in life.

After completing his medical school training, Frankl developed his ideas while serving as a school counselor as well as in the suicide

---

[91] Catholic Church and John Paul. *Encyclical Letter, Fides Et Ratio, of the Supreme Pontiff John Paul II: To the Bishops of the Catholic Church on the Relationship between Faith and Reason* (Washington, D.C.: United States Catholic Conference, 1998), p. 4.

[92] Logotherapy is discussed in further detail below.

ward of a general hospital in Vienna. In 1940, he was made the head of the department of neurology at the Rothschild Hospital, the only hospital for Jews in Vienna after it had been occupied by the Nazis. While there, Frankl made many false diagnoses of patients in order to circumvent hospital regulations requiring euthanasia of the mentally ill. He continued to develop some of his own ideas for psychology and psychiatry, and consolidated many of his notes into a manuscript for a book that he entitled *The Doctor and the Soul*.[93]

In 1942, in part as a consequence of his protection of Jews at Rothschild Hospital, Frankl was arrested along with his wife, father, and brother and taken to a concentration camp in Bohemia. He was later transferred to Auschwitz. During his time in the camps, Frankl began to observe that those prisoners who chose to seek and hold onto meaning for their lives, despite their seemingly hopeless circumstances, flourished more than those who gave themselves over in desperation to the apparent meaninglessness of their existence. As he observed these differing mental, emotional and spiritual states, Frankl began to develop his notion of "will to meaning." He later recalled:

> We had to learn ourselves, and, furthermore, we had to teach the despairing men, that *it did not really matter what we expected from life, but rather what life expected from us.* We needed to stop asking about the meaning of life, and instead to think of ourselves as those who were being questioned by life - daily and hourly. Our answer must consist, not in talk and meditation, but in right action and in right conduct. Life ultimately means taking the responsibility to find the right answer to its

---

[93] The manuscript was eventually published, as noted below, as Viktor E. Frankl, *The Doctor and the Soul: from Psychotherapy to Logotherapy.* (New York: Vintage Books, 1986).

problems and to fulfill the tasks which it constantly sets for each individual. These tasks, and therefore the meaning of life, differ from man to man, and from moment to moment. [italics in original][94]

Frankl was given the opportunity to put his own theory to the test. During his transfer from Bohemia to Auschwitz, Frankl had tried to hide his manuscript for his book by sewing it into the lining of his coat, but was forced to discard it at the last minute. The manuscript was eventually discovered and destroyed. Meanwhile, Frankl spent most of the time during the remaining years of his incarceration attempting to remember and recite his manuscript, scribbling notes on stolen scraps of paper whenever possible, so that he could re-create it at the conclusion of the war. This project, which had been his life's work prior to the war, sustained him through the war and through the dark days after his release when he discovered that his wife and most of his relatives had been killed by the Nazis.

Will to Meaning

This "will to meaning" (*der Will zum Zinn*) as observed in others, and as experienced personally, was for Frankl so essential and critical to human existence that it is all but a requirement for life. Will to meaning can also provide sufficient reason for heroic action that could lead to death:

> Man's search for meaning is the primary motivation in his life and not a "secondary rationalization" of instinctual drives. This meaning is unique and specific in that it must and can be fulfilled by him alone; only

---

[94] Viktor E. Frankl, *Man's Search for Meaning: An Introduction to Logotherapy*, (Boston: Beacon Press, 1992), p. 85.

then does it achieve a significance which will satisfy his own will to meaning. There are some authors who will contend that meanings and values are "nothing but defense mechanisms, reaction formations, and sublimations." But as for myself, I would not be willing to live merely for the sake of my "defense mechanisms," nor would I be ready to die merely for the sake of my "reaction formations."[95]

According to Frankl, the primary need of each human being is to find a purpose for his or her personal existence, that is:

a sense of significance in the totality of experience that marks him as a unique individual, different from all others in the entire history of the world.[96]

When he finds this, Frankl holds, he can go on against all odds; when he lacks it, he feels empty and frustrated in spite of whatever else he may have.

Frankl encouraged therapists to ask probing questions that elicited patients' sense of purpose in life, and to explore patients' understanding of and commitment to such purpose. Therapists were trained to listen for indications of meaninglessness, and to pursue those signals in order to uncover the extent to which a lack of purpose or meaning contributed to such symptoms as anxiety, boredom or depression. Therapists made particular use of two techniques: de-reflection and paradoxical intent. De-reflection was a technique that involved redirecting the patient's attention away from outward symptoms and toward another person or a source of meaning. Paradoxical intent was a technique of symptom prescription,

---

[95] Frankl, *Man's Search for Meaning*, p. 105.
[96] James C. Crumbaugh, "Frankl's Logotherapy: A New Orientation in Meaning." *Journal of Religion and Health*. 10 no. 4 (October 1971): 376.

that is, asking the patient to deliberately increase an outward reaction such as anxiety or sweating, if only to demonstrate the futility of obsessing over such symptoms as an underlying sense of purposelessness.

In some respects, his emphasis on will to meaning was Frankl's response to the prevailing notions of will to pleasure (the ultimate human quest as posited by Sigmund Freud) and will to power (the ultimate human quest as posited by Adler).[97] For Freud (1856-1939), the human being is a pleasure-seeking animal that responds to instinctive *libido* or sexual energy. For Alfred Adler (1870-1937), the human being is a control-seeking animal that respond to an instinctive need for mastery. In respect of his third way, Frankl's logotherapy has been designated the Third Viennese School of Psychotherapy, following after Freud ("First School") and Adler ("Second School").[98]

The Power of Purpose

"Meaning in life" and "purpose in life" have often been used interchangeably.[99] However, taken literally, "meaning" seems to imply a broader, more foundational concept, while "purpose" would seem to imply a narrower goal-orientation that may or may not emanate from meaning. As such, meaning may inform purpose or purposefulness and provide the raw material with which purpose is constructed.[100]

---

[97] Amanda M.A. Melton and Stefan E. Schulenberg. "On the Measurement of Meaning: Logotherapy's Empirical Contributions to Humanistic Psychology." *The Humanistic Psychologist*, 36 (2008): 33.

[98] Robert C. Barnes, "Viktor Frankl's Logotherapy: Spirituality and Meaning in the New Millennium," *Texas Counseling Association Journal.* 28, no. 1 (Spring 2000): 24.

[99] *See* William Damon, Jenni Menon, and Kendall Cotton Bronk. "The Development of Purpose During Adolescence" *Applied Developmental Science* 7, no. 3 (July 2003): 121. The terms "meaning" and "purpose" are often used interchangeably, as they were by Victor Frankl and other researchers.

[100] *Ibid*, p. 121. In their review of the social science literature, the authors conclude that "purpose is seen to be one subset of meaning." They define purpose as "a stable

As a practical matter, a loss of purpose in life seems to carry with it a loss of meaning in life. Together, purposelessness and meaninglessness result in a frustration of the will to meaning and create an inner void that Frankl called an *existential vacuum*.[101] When he surveyed his college students, Frankl discovered that 25% of his European students, and as many as 60% of his American students, showed a more-or-less marked degree of such existential vacuum.[102] Frankl theorized that this resulted "from a frustration of our existential needs which in turn has become a universal phenomenon in our industrial societies."[103]

From a more technical or psychological perspective, Frankl theorized that existential frustration occurs when the search for meaning is thwarted. If neurotic symptoms occur because of existential frustration, this is called "noögenic neurosis." Symptoms of noögenic neurosis include evidence of existential despair – which is usually expressed as boredom[104] – and a sense of simply "going through the motions" of life.[105] As one researcher summed up this phenomenon:

---

and generalized intention to accomplish something that is at once meaningful to the self and consequential to the world beyond the self."

[101] Frankl, *Man's Search for Meaning*, p. 111. Frankl concluded that people who suffer from such existential vacuum experience a feeling of "total and ultimate meaninglessness of their lives." *Ibid*, p. 110.

[102] *Ibid*, p. 129.

[103] *Ibid*, p. 141.

[104] James C. Crumbaugh and Leonard T. Maholick. "An Experimental Study in Existentialism: The Psychometric Approach to Frankl's Concept of Noögenic Neurosis" *Journal of Clinical Psychology* (1964): 589. "Noögenic" is derived from *nous*, the Greek word pertaining to the spiritual and aspirational qualities of the human mind.

[105] Stefan E. Schulenberg, Robert R. Hutzell, Carrie Nassif and Julius M. Rogina. "Logotherapy for Clinical Practice." *Psychotherapy: Theory, Research, Practice, Training*, 45, no. 4 (2008): 449.

The person is the center of a personal universe where nothing happens – the scenery outside changes and people pass by, and that is all. There are no beginnings, there is no exit, and the only relationship that can be established is that of being in the way. The person has no right to exist – he is a zero. In attempting to overcome his despair, the person denies any claims on him from the outside, denies the necessity for making decisions, and through provisional living, fatalism, collective thinking, or fanaticism, denies that meaning is worth finding, possible to find, or personal. In short, existential despair is an experience of helplessness to feel significant and have an impact on others, or simply, powerlessness.[106]

According to Frankl, these feelings of meaninglessness are often behind "the mass neurotic triad of today, i.e., depression-addiction-aggression."[107]

Frankl's logotherapy was articulated and prescribed in several publications, starting with *Man's Search for Meaning.*[108] Frankl meant for his psychotherapy to provide aid, if not a cure, for those suffering from depression or other disorders that stemmed from a perceived loss of purpose or meaning in life. He proposed that life does not necessarily have meaning, or a purpose, in and of itself, but that purpose in life is specific to the individual and must emerge from the circumstances of each person's immediate life. As people engage

---

[106] Kirk E.Farnsworth. "Despair that Restores" *Psychotherapy: Theory, Research & Practice* 12, no. 1 (Spring 1975): 45.

[107] Frankl, *Doctor and the Soul*, p. 298.

[108] Frankl, *Man's Search for Meaning*, p. 85.

and are engaged by life's experiences and environment, they find themselves moving toward existential vacuum (i. e., no meaning) or toward purpose in life (i. e., meaning). The key to logotherapy is the recognition of these dynamics and the volitional choice to seek, or not seek, meaning.

Frankl's ideas have formed the basis for several instruments used by social science researchers for measuring subjects' sense of meaning in life and, inversely, existential boredom. The most common measure of the former has been the *Purpose in Life Test* (PIL) developed by James C. Crumbaugh and Leonard T. Maholick[109]. The latter is generally measured by use of the *Boredom Proneness Scale* developed by Richard Farmer and Norman Sundberg.[110]

As might be expected, the PIL correlates positively with constructs such as happiness, emotional stability, and extroversion, and negatively with constructs such as boredom proneness, anxiety, and depression.[111] In other words, when people have a sense of meaning and purpose in life, they tend to be more content with life; when the opposite is true, they tend to be bored and anxious and depressed[112]. The PIL and related instruments have been used to show that a lack of purpose in life has been statistically associated with suicide

[109] *See* James C. Crumbaugh and Leonard T. Maholick, *Manual of Instructions for the Purpose-in- Life Test* (Munster, Ind.: Psychometric Affiliates, 1969).

[110] *See* Richard Farmer and Norman Sundberg. "Boredom Proneness—The Development and Correlates of a New Scale". *Journal of Personality Assessment* 50, no. 1 (1986): 4-17.

[111] *See* Robert R. Hutzell, "A Review of the Purpose in Life Test," *The International Forum for Logotherapy* 11 (1988): 89–101.

[112] Rostyslaw W. Robak and Paul W. Griffin, "Purpose in Life: What is its Relationship to Happiness, Depression, and Grieving?" *North American Journal of Psychology* 2, no. 1 (2000): 113-119; and Dominique Louis Debats, Petra M. Van der Lubbe and Fimmy R.A. Wezeman, "On the Psychometric Properties of the Life Regard Index (LRI): A Measure of Meaningful Life," *Personality and Individual Differences* 14, no. 2 (February 1993): 337-345.

ideation and attempts,[113] mid-life crisis symptoms,[114] and feelings of hopelessness.[115]

Irvin D. Yalom (b. 1931), an existential psychotherapist on the faculty of Stanford University, has studied the PIL and its findings over time. His 1980 summary of the PIL led him to the conclusion that the test corroborates the following:

1. Lack of meaning in life is associated with psychopathology in a roughly linear sense: that is, the less the sense of meaning, the greater the severity of psychopathology.
2. A positive sense of meaning in life is associated with deeply held religious beliefs.
3. A positive life meaning is associated with self-transcendent values.
4. A positive sense of meaning in life is associated with membership in groups, dedication to some cause, and adoption of clear life goals.
5. Life meaning must be viewed in a developmental perspective: the types of life meaning change over an individual's life;

---

[113] Lisa L. Harlow, Michael D. Newcomb, and P.M. Bentler, "Depression, Self-derogation, Substance Use, and Suicide Ideation: Lack of Purpose in Life as a Mediational Factor," *Journal of Clinical Psychology* 42, no. 1 (January 1986): 5-21; and David Lester and Souhel Badro, "Depression, Suicidal Preoccupation and Purpose in Life in a Subclinical Population," *Personality and Individual Differences* 13, no. 1 (1992): 75-76.

[114] Daniel T.L. Shek, "Meaning in Life and Adjustment in Midlife Parents in Hong Kong," *International Forum for Logotherapy* 17, no. 2 (1994): 102-107.

[115] Daniel T.L. Shek, "Measurement in Pessimism in Chinese Adolescents: The Chinese Hopelessness Scale," *Social Behavior and Personality*, 21, no. 2 (1993): 107-119.

other developmental tasks must precede development of meaning.[116]

Logotherapy, and its focus on addressing the root problem of purposelessness, has been developed to the point where specific logotherapy protocols are used by therapists to treat specific conditions. Recent World Congresses on Logotherapy have included paper presentations proposing the incorporation of logotherapy into the treatment of specific diagnoses of the *Diagnostic and Statistical Manual of Mental Disorders* (DSM–IV–TR).[117] For example, a recent paper included proposed logotherapy applications for the treatment of mood disorders, anxiety disorders, and personality disorders.[118]

Even though logotherapy is more or less an existentialist or humanistic approach to therapy, it is also considered by many to be a subset or example of several cognitive psychotherapeutic approaches.[119] Logotherapy, more recently referred to as meaning therapy,[120] continues to be explored as an appropriate treatment for an expanding and increasingly diverse variety of situations, ranging from marital

---

[116] Irvin D. Yalom. *Existential Psychotherapy* (New York: Basic Books, 1980): 459-460.

[117] American Psychiatric Association. *Diagnostic and Statistical Manual of Mental Disorders DSM-IV-TR.* (Arlington, VA: American Psychiatric Assoc, 2010).

[118] *See* Stefan E. Schulenberg, Robert R. Hutzell, Carrie Nassif and Julius M. Rogina. "Logotherapy for Clinical Practice," *Psychotherapy: Theory, Research, Practice, Training* 45, no. 4 (December 2008): 447-463.

[119] Michael J. Mahoney, "Introduction to Special Section: Theoretical Developments in Cognitive Psychotherapies," *Journal of Consulting and Clinical Psychology* 61, no. 2 (1993): 188; *See* Dagmar Devorah Sigrid Fabry, Alia Sheikh and Matthew Selman, "Logotherapy can Enrich Cognitive Behavioral Therapy Practice," *The International Forum for Logotherapy* 30 (2007): 100-106.

[120] Paul T.P. Wong. "Meaning Therapy: An Integrative and Positive Existential Psychotherapy". *Journal of Contemporary Psychotherapy.* 40, no. 2 (2010): 85-93.

conflict[121] to obesity[122] to post-traumatic stress disorder.[123] Indeed, logotherapy has been considered a subset of a "third wave" of cognitive behavioral therapy known as "act and commitment therapy."[124]

Logotherapy researchers and other social scientists have also confirmed through empirical studies the seemingly intuitive notion that the loss of hope triggers a loss of meaning and purpose. Hope, in turn, is a concept that involves time. It involves the future. As psychologist Henri F. Ellenberger observed:

> Normally, we look upon the future not only for itself but also for compensating and correcting the past and the present. We reckon on the future for paying our debts, achieving success, enjoying life, becoming good Christians. Wherever the future becomes empty, as with manics and certain psychopaths, life is a perpetual gamble and the advantage of the present minute is taken into consideration; wherever the future is inaccessible or blocked, as it is with the depressed, hope necessarily disappears and life loses all meaning.[125]

[121] *See* Stefan E. Schulenberg, Lindsay W. Schnetzer, Michael R. Winters and Robert R. Hutzell, "Meaning-Centered Couples Therapy: Logotherapy and Intimate Relationships," *Journal of Contemporary Psychotherapy* 40 (2010): 95-102.

[122] *See* Moshe Mishali, Ronit Endevelt, and Anthony D. Heymann. "The 'Emphatic Narrative': A New Tool for Obesity Treatment". *Nutrition Today*. 46, no. 1 (2010): 27-32.

[123] *See* Fredrike P. Bannink. "Posttraumatic Success: Solution-Focused Brief Therapy". *Brief Treatment and Crisis Intervention*. 8, no. 3 (2008): 215-225.

[124] Lily A. Brown, Brandon A. Gaudiano, and Ivan W. Miller. "Investigating the Similarities and Differences between Practitioners of Second- and Third-Wave Cognitive-Behavioral Therapies". *Behavior Modification* 35, no. 2 (2011): 187-200.

[125] Henri F. Ellenberger, "A Clinical Introduction to Psychiatric Phenomenology and Existential Analysis." In May, Rollo, and Ludwig Binswanger. *Existence; a New Dimension in Psychiatry and Psychology* (New York: Basic Books, 1958): 106-107.

Finding a Purpose

Logotherapy, meaning therapy, cognitive reparative therapy, and the variations on these techniques, are helpful to patients because they address an essential and chronic problem, that is, meaninglessness, purposelessness, or existential vacuum. Those conditions, which can occur in the midst of a pampered, trouble-free, carefree lifestyle as often or more often than otherwise, frequently lead to boredom and depression. The psychotherapeutic approaches discussed here tend to help patients find, or even create, meaning and purpose in life to help them cope with life.

If purposelessness is the problem, what is the solution? While the specific avenues to meaningfulness vary from therapist to therapist as well as from patient to patient, there are certain categories of such avenues that emerge from the literature. Faith is one category, and it will be addressed separately below. Aside from faith *per se*, Kobus de Smidt suggests that the following are the primary avenues to purpose in life that tend to occur as a result of meaning-based psychotherapies: creative values, encounters and experiences, and attitudinal values.[126]

To find meaning in creative values is to pour oneself into unique tasks and to be committed to such tasks. Work, hobbies, development of greater appreciation for art and beauty, community service, development of relationships with others, development of a rootedness with a place (or the earth and its environment), ministry or spirituality, and commitment to a political or charitable cause are typical projects that allow for purpose and meaning. It is the giving of oneself to such a project outside of oneself that allows the individual to find meaning. It is meaning derived from intentional activity, such as service to others.

---

[126] Kobus de Smidt, "The Human Freedom to Find Meaning: A Logo-Philosophical Reading of Revelation 1:3," *Missionalia* 33, no. 3 (November 2005): 513-514.

For Frankl, the specific task is much less important than how one contextualizes and responds to the task.

Encounters and experiences allow for individuals to discover the good, the true, and the beautiful. This can occur through a commitment to experience something, such as art, or nature or world travel. Or, more often, it can come through the encountering of others, by giving and receiving love. It is meaning derived from awe or from relationship.

The reconstruction of attitudinal values involves a purposeful change in the stand humans take toward their circumstances and their sufferings. Particularly in hopeless situations, self transcendence can occur when individuals not only accept their circumstances for what they are (that is, beyond control), but accept the possibility that suffering, and even the seemingly unconditional meaninglessness of life, can itself have meaning. It is meaning derived from philosophical reassessment.

Two cases of adults who were molested as children and who underwent logotherapy can serve as examples of how meaning-making can make a difference. The cases are reported by Jim and Jan Lantz, two social workers affiliated with the Ohio State University College of Social Work, in a 1992 issue of the *Journal of Religion and Health*.[127] The first case involved "Sandy", who was suffering from nightmares and was showing symptoms of depression. The second case involved "Mary", who was experiencing anxiety attacks and having difficulty managing many aspects of her life. Upon entering logotherapy, both Sandy and Mary scored 86 on the Purpose in Life Test.

As part of her logotherapy, Sandy took some steps to resolve her troubled history, including filing a criminal complaint against the neighbor who molested her during her youth, and having serious

---

[127] Jim Lantz and Jan Lantz, "Franklian Psychotherapy with Adults Molested as Children," *Journal of Religion and Health* 42, no. 4 (Winter 1992): 297-304.

discussions with her parents who had somehow been unaware of the problem at the time. She also discovered that she had an excellent ability to listen to other women who had been molested or raped, and became a volunteer at a local rape crisis center. Sandy recommitted herself to her marriage and went through a second wedding ceremony with her husband. After several years of therapy, Sandy's score on the Purpose in Life Test was 124, and she scored 125 at her four-year follow-up evaluation.

Mary also resolved some of the issues that were keeping her from making progress on her college degree and from having solid social relationships. Mary started volunteering to assist abused children at a local child welfare agency "in honor" of her own lost childhood. She also became a Big Sister to an adolescent who had been removed from an abusive home, and began volunteering in several other capacities. She made a long-term commitment to helping abused and neglected children, and accepted a job as an accountant at a child welfare agency. After several years, Mary's score on the Purpose in Life Test was 129, and she scored 126 at her three-year follow-up evaluation.

In the end, meaning-based psychotherapies are designed to help patients discover that meaning in life comes from life itself. In other words, each person is encouraged to develop an expectation that the totality of life's experience has a greater overall significance than can be immediately perceived by the individual. According to Frankl, people are hard-wired with a "will to meaning," and meaning-based psychotherapies tap into and foster this impulse so that purpose can be created or discovered.

Roadblocks to Meaning-Seeking

Maslow's Conditions Precedent to Self-Actualization and Transcendence

Abraham Maslow (1908–1970) studied and developed theories about human drives, motivations, and the ways in which people reach their human potential. He concluded that people are driven toward self-actualization and transcendence. That is, people seek ultimate meaning for their work and their lives by engaging in a project of attempting to achieve their fullest potential as human beings. He described self-actualization as follows:

> It refers to the person's desire for self-fulfillment, namely, to the tendency for him to become actualized in what he is potentially. The specific form that these needs will take will of course vary greatly from person to person. In one individual it may take the form of the desire to be an ideal mother, in another it may be expressed athletically, and in still another it may be expressed in painting pictures or in inventions.[128]

A key element of Maslow's analysis was his observation that to some extent there are conditions precedent to the progression toward self-actualization and transcendence. In particular, he observed that the individual's concerns about his or her larger purpose in life can be trumped and pushed to the background by immediate physiological needs such as food and safety. Maslow postulated that humans are driven to meet their more basic needs, such as physiological needs and safety, before they can strive for self-actualization:

---

[128] Abraham Maslow, "A theory of human motivation," *Psychological Review* 50 (1943): 382.

It is quite true that man lives by bread alone - when there is no bread. But what happens to man's desires when there is plenty of bread and when his belly is chronically filled? *At once other (and "higher") needs emerge* and these, rather than physiological hungers, dominate the organism. And when these in turn are satisfied, again new (and still "higher") needs emerge and so on. This is what we mean by saying that the basic human needs are organized into a hierarchy of relative prepotency.[129]

Maslow's hierarchical model continues to enjoy broad support among psychology researchers and scholars today. For example, a comprehensive research-based taxonomy of human goals recently developed by Chulef, Read and Walsh revealed a number of interesting parallels with Maslow's theoretical classifications of human motivators:[130]

For example, Maslow's Physiological (or Biological) needs are similar to this study's Physical and Sexual goals; his Security and Safety needs are captured by this taxonomy's needs for Stability, Safety, Security, and the Avoidance of negative situations, his Affiliation (or Attachment) needs tap into Interpersonal goals such as Friendship, Belonging/Social recognition/Approval, and Receiving from others, and his cognitive needs resemble our taxonomy's Intellectual, Educational, and Creativity-related goals. Finally, Maslow's

[129] *Ibid*, 375.
[130] Ada S. Chulef, Stephen J. Read and David A. Walsh, "A Hierarchical Taxonomy of Human Goals," *Motivation and Emotion* 25, no. 3 (September 2001): 191-232.

Self-actualization need tends to relate to Intrapersonal goals referring to Self-determination and Personal growth, and his Transcendence needs tend to relate to this taxonomy's "finding higher meaning," "mature understanding," and "life's limitations."[131]

To suggest that anyone whose physiological needs are met is necessarily motivated to progress toward transcendence would be a misinterpretation and misapplication of Maslow's theory. But it is intuitive and almost self-evident that larger aspirations in regard to meaning and purpose in life are unlikely to be forefront in the mind of a person who is starving or in desperate need of water or sleep. Similarly, there can be other stressors (such as health issues, debts, family or personal relationship problems, loss of income, etc.) that can overwhelm an individual to the point where his or her anxieties inhibit motivation and the ability to give thoughtful consideration to life's purpose or meaning.

Self-Directedness Inhibitors

Self-directedness is an attribute that takes into account coping skills (i.e., acquiring the necessary information, skills or assistance for coping with stressors in life) and a willingness to improve. Self-directedness reflects some degree of self-acceptance, the acceptance of personal responsibility, and the perception of the self as somewhat autonomous and integrated. Some researchers, like Rasmussen and Den Uyl, hold a very high view of self-directedness, considering this trait to be:

---

[131] *Ibid*,p. 224.

both a necessary condition for self-perfection and a necessary feature of all self-perfecting acts at whatever level of achievement or development — what we have called the very form in which human flourishing exists ...[132]

To the extent that self-directedness represents the willingness of an individual to improve himself or herself, however, it can be inhibited or blocked. One category of inhibitors to self-directedness is that of personality disorders: individuals with personality disorders tend to have low self-directedness.

The *Diagnostic and Statistical Manual of Mental Disorders IV* defines personality disorders in terms of enduring patterns of perceiving, relating to, and thinking about the environment and oneself that are inflexible and maladaptive, and which cause significant functional impairment or subjective distress (American Psychiatric Association, 2000:686).[133] Of course, some symptoms of personality disorders may be more properly explained by substance abuse, injuries such as head trauma, Alzheimer's disease, dementia, malnutrition or other medical conditions. Absent such conditions, personality orders *per se* may inhibit a person's propensity to engage in meaning-seeking or philosophical inquiry.

One grouping of personality disorders is denominated *Cluster A* and refers to "low reward dependence" disorders that exhibit low self-directedness. Cluster A includes personality disorders that result in an odd or eccentric social image, including Paranoid Personality Disorder, Schizoid Personality Disorder, and Schizotypal Personality

---

[132] Douglas B. Rasmussen, and Douglas J. Den Uyl. *Liberty and Nature: An Aristotelian Defense of Liberal Order* (La Salle, Ill: Open Court, 1991): 95.
[133] American Psychiatric Association, *Diagnostic and Statistical Manual of Mental Disorders: DSM-IV-TR*, (Arlington, VA: American Psychiatric Assoc., 2010): 686.

Disorder. These disorders are self-focused and tend to interfere with an individual's ability or motivation to develop an expansive view of life or meaning in life.

A second grouping of personality disorders is denominated *Cluster B* and refers to "low reward dependence" disorders that also exhibit low self-directedness. Cluster B refers to people who are overly dramatic, emotionally labile and erratic, including Antisocial Personality Disorder, Borderline Personality Disorder, Histrionic Personality Disorder, and Narcissistic Personality Disorder.

A third grouping of personality disorders is denominated *Cluster -C* and refers to "high harm avoidance" disorders that also exhibit low self-directedness. Cluster C includes disorders that describe people who are typically anxious or fearful across social situations, including Avoidant Personality Disorder, Dependent Personality Disorder, and Obsessive-Compulsive Personality Disorder. There are some indications that individuals afflicted with *Cluster C* disorders may be more open to seeking assistance and resolution than those afflicted with *Cluster A* disorders.[134]

In addition to personality disorders, other inhibitors of self-directedness can include traumatic brain injuries,[135] attention deficit hyperactivity disorder (ADHD),[136] borderline personality

---

[134] Peter Tyrer, Sarah Mitchard, Caroline Methuen, and Maja Ranger, "Treatment Rejecting and Treatment Seeking Personality Disorders: Type R and Type S," *Journal of Personality Disorders 17*, no. 3 (2003): 264.

[135] Elizabeth Kendall, "Psychosocial Adjustment Following Closed Head Injury: A Model for Understanding Individual Differences and Predicting Outcome," *Neuropsychological Rehabilitation: An International Journal* 6, no. 2 (1996): 111-112.

[136] *See* Russell A. Barkley, *Taking Charge of Adult ADHD* (New York: Guilford Press, 2010).

organization,[137] Asperger syndrome,[138] etc. As in the case of Maslow's model, the research seems to indicate that preconditions to self-directedness include a minimal level of intellectual, emotional, and neuropychological normalcy and health. Absent these preconditions, self-directedness and any attendant notion of meaning-seeking or purpose-seeking are likely to be inhibited.

Lack of Ultimate Purpose: Hyperboredom and Dread

Less Purpose Means More Boredom

There is a difference between not having *a* purpose (which results in an existential frustration of the universal will to meaning), and not having ultimate purpose. The former is a baseline, a minimum floor of practical purposefulness that meets certain psychological and emotional needs; it lends itself to psychotherapeutic intervention. The latter is not so much a ceiling than the removal of the ceiling; it is less easily addressed through therapy.

Frankl concluded that not having any purpose can trigger existential frustration or noögenic neurosis, which in turn can result in aggression, addiction, or depression, but he also observed that part of, or an extension of, the will to meaning is the will to ultimate meaning. Ultimate meaning, in turn, requires more depth, more substance, and more spiritual or metaphysical significance than meaningfulness proper or purposefulness proper.

The main problem with the pursuit of ultimate meaning, though,

---

[137] Otto F. Kernberg, "A psychoanalytic model for the classification of personality disorders," In M. Achenheil, B. Bondy, R. Engel, M. Ermann, & N. Nedopil (Eds.), *Implications of Psychopharmacology to Psychiatry: Biological, Nosological, and Therapeutical Concepts* (New York: Springer, 1996): 71.

[138] Henrik Soderstrom, Maria Rastam and Christopher Gillberg, "Temperament and Character in Adults with Asperger Syndrome," *Autism* 6, no.3 (2002): 290.

is that it is elusive. For some it may be impossible, even though it is central to existence.[139] Indeed, Frankl admitted that even though a life committed to the quest for ultimate meaning is a life lived to the fullest, "the more comprehensive the meaning, the less comprehensible it is."[140]

On the other hand, empirical research has shown that being bored tends to be inversely related to having a sense of purpose in life. In other words, the more meaning and purpose that an individual has in life, the less boredom he or she will experience. Studies of both elderly people[141] and youth[142] have demonstrated this negative correlation.

Meaninglessness and Hyperboredom

Just as there seemed to Frankl and other meaning-based therapists that there are different levels or intensities of existential frustration or existential vacuum, there are different types of boredom. Seán Desmond Healy (b. 1927) did an extensive historical analysis of boredom and differentiated between three kinds of boredom: boredom$_1$, boredom$_2$ and boredom$_3$[143]. Boredom$_1$ is a transient annoyance with a clearly identifiable, if temporary, external cause such as performing a repetitive

---

[139] *See* Joseph Fabry, "The Calls of Meaning," in *The Human Quest for Meaning: A Handbook of Psychological Research and Clinical Applications*, edited by Wong, Paul T. P., and Prem S. Fry (Mahwah, N.J.: Lawrence Erlbaum Associates, 1998): 298.

[140] Viktor E. Frankl, *Man's Search for Ultimate Meaning* (New York: Insight Books, 1997): 143.

[141] *See* Lawrence Weinstein, Xiaolin Xie, and Charalambos C. Cleanthous, "Purpose in Life, Boredom and Volunteerism in a Group of Retirees," *Psychological Reports* 76, no. 2 (April 1995): 482.

[142] *See* Amanda M.A. Melton and Stefan E. Schulenberg, "On the Relationship between Meaning in Life and Boredom Proneness: Examining a Logotherapy Postulate," *Psychological Reports* 101, no. 3F (December 2007): 1016-1022.

[143] Seán Desmond Healy, *Boredom, Self, and Culture* (Rutherford: Fairleigh Dickinson University Press, 1984): 42-57.

task or having to be immobile for a length of time. Boredom$_2$ is also transient, but represents a vague restlessness that may be connected with a lack of things to do, but that is not necessarily tied to a specific cause or condition.

Boredom$_3$ is a chronic state which Healy calls "hyperboredom" and is associated with distress, dread, a loss of meaning in life, or some combination of these. According to Healy, hyperboredom involves a greater level of compulsion and dysphoria than the more temporary or transient types.[144] It is a profound loss of one's sense of place in space and time, a condition that Martin Heidegger (1889-1976) described as follows:

> This profound boredom, drifting hither and thither in the abysses of existence like a mute fog, draws all things, all men and oneself along with them, together in a queer kind of indifference. This boredom reveals what-is in totality.[145]

Hyperboredom as a symptom of a lack of ultimate meaning is a phenomenon that Healy traces throughout history,[146] and shows that it is a phenomenon that is less connected to stress and the pressures and exigencies of life, than to leisure:

> The idea that leisure leads to boredom is one that can be traced back at least two millennia; to Horace, for example, urging the need for manual labor to combat its effects; to Seneca, writing of leisure as a "vice," and warning one of his correspondents that "it must

---

[144] *Ibid*, p. 67.
[145] Martin Heidegger, "What is Metaphysics" in *Existence and Being*, Translated by Werner Brock (Chicago: H. Regnery Co, 1949): 121.
[146] Healy, *Boredom*, pp. 85-88.

be shaken off by occupation"; to similar warnings in the Old and New Testaments, from the book of Ecclesiasticus [sic] to the letters of St. Paul.[147]

If Adler's "will to power" provides some indication of the human need to control circumstances in order to achieve stability, comfort and pleasure, then history seems to suggest that hyperboredom (or "sheer boredom") can be expected as the ultimate outcome.

There are two typical responses to boredom of all kinds: sensation-seeking (i.e., an effort to increase stimulation of pleasure), and meaning seeking (i.e., an effort to increase meaning and purpose in life). However, they eventually become conflated as the physical and sensual capacities for sensation-seeking are exhausted, and sensation-seeking eventually leads to and merges with meaning-seeking. This is the grand ennui described in Ecclesiastes 1:1-11, and which has been observed in the lives of the rich and powerful throughout history. As Lewis Mumford (1895-1990) observed:

> Nothing is more striking throughout history than the chronic disaffection, the malaise, the anxiety, and the psychotic self-destructiveness of the ruling classes, once they are in command of "all that the heart can desire." For the dominant minority, the privileged few, have always been faced with the ultimate curse of such a meaningless existence: sheer boredom.[148]

The curse of sheer boredom is not visited solely upon the rich and the powerful, the privileged few, or the ruling classes. It is universal.

---

[147] *Ibid*, p. 85.
[148] Lewis Mumford, *The Pentagon of Power* (New York: Harcourt Brace Jovanovich, 1970): 342.

The very condition of man, Pascal notes, is "inconstancy, weariness, unrest."[149] Healy references the pithy observation of Edmund Bergler:

> Even if we felt quite safe on every side, boredom on its own account... would not fail to emerge from the depths of our hearts where it is naturally rooted, and poison our whole mind. Man is so unhappy that he would be bored even if he had no cause for boredom, by the very nature of his temperament.[150]

Meaninglessness and Generalized Anxiety

Boredom, hyper- or otherwise, and whether triggered by a lack of purpose or not, causes anxiety. People do not desire to be bored, and when they are, they complain about it. In other words, boredom results in anxiety, even if the boredom is merely the transient types of boredom described by Healy as boredom$_1$ and boredom$_2$.

Purposelessness and meaninglessness, in turn, produce generalized anxiety, even if that anxiety is not necessarily associated with existential vacuum or boredom. As one researcher wrote:

> The human brain can not sustain purposeless living. It was not designed for that. Its systems are designed for purposive actions, and when blocked, they deteriorate, and the emotional feedback from idling those systems

---

[149] Blaise Pascal, *Pensées* S58/L23/B127, trans. Roger Ariew (Indianapolis, IN: Hackett Publishing Co., 2005):10. Citations to *Pensées* include references to fragments as organized by Sellier (reflected in Pascal and Ariew, *supra*), LaFuma (*see* Blaise Pascal, *Pensées*, trans. A.J. Kraisheimer. [London: Penguin Books, 1995]), and Brunschvicg (*see* Blaise Pascal, *Pensées*, trans. W.F. Trotter [Mineola, NY: Dover Publications, 2003]), respectively. Page numbers refer to Pascal and Ariew, *supra*.
[150] Edmund Bergler, "On the Disease-Entity Boredom ("Alysosis") and its Psychopathology," *Psychiatric Quarterly* 19, no. 1 (January 1945): 51.

signals extreme discomfort and motivates the search for renewed purpose and hence meaning.[151]

Finding meaning in life reduces anxiety, even if the meaning that is found can be viewed as dysfunctional or worse: even those who find meaning in, for example, a life of crime, exhibit less anxiety than criminals who do not.[152]

Meaning-Seeking and Faith

The notions of meaning and purpose necessarily have metaphysical, and even spiritual, qualities.[153] A person's philosophical presuppositions or worldview regarding the metaphysical and regarding a transcendent ideal, presence or Person, will necessarily shape the way in which that person finds meaning. And vice-versa. The quest for meaning may motivate a search that leads to faith, but faith once found can serve to redefine meaning and what it means to seek meaning in the first place.[154]

Indeed, the more faith-oriented a person is, the more likely

---

[151] Eric Klinger, "The Search for Meaning in Evolutionary Perspective and Its Clinical Implications," in *The Human Quest for Meaning: A Handbook of Psychological Research and Clinical Applications* edited by Wong, Paul T. P. and Prem S. Fry (Mahwah, N.J.: Lawrence Erlbaum Associates, 1998): 33.

[152] Moshe Addad, "Psychogenic Neuroticism and Noogenic Self-Strengthening," *Internaional Forum for Logotherapy*. 10 (1987): 52-59.

[153] As noted above at note 27, Irvin Yalom's survey of the results of the Purpose in Life test as reported in the literature indicated that a positive sense of meaning in life is associated with deeply held religious beliefs and is also associated with self-transcendent values.

[154] *See* R. Ruard Ganzevoort, "Theory and Practice - Religious Coping Reconsidered, Part One: An Integrated Approach," *Journal of Psychology and Theology* 26, no. 3 (1998): 260-275; and R. Ruard Ganzevoort "Theory and Practice - Religious Coping Reconsidered, Part Two: A Narrative Reformulation". *Journal of Psychology and Theology* 26, no. 3 (1998): 276-286.

that person will not only find meaning, but will be more likely to flourish psychologically and even physically. For example, research has found strong positive correlations between spiritually-informed meaningfulness and the mental, physical and emotional well-being of HIV/AIDS patients[155] as well as kidney transplant patients[156]. The very fact that a person finds meaning within a spiritual framework (rather than a merely naturalistic or secular framework) provides that person with a larger, more magnificent, and hardier outlook, because spirituality:

> Leads the person to think in terms of a higher order of functioning that emphasizes honesty, justice, courage, altruism, and other values, thus facilitating transcendence of experiential specifics through efforts to improve functioning and search for positive meaning in life.[157]

For his part, Frankl insisted that his meaning-centered concepts comprised a solely secular approach to psychotherapy.[158] Nevertheless,

---

[155] Kelly M. Trevino, Kenneth I. Pargament, Sian Cotton, Anthony C. Leonard, June Hahn, Caron Ann Caprini-Faigin, and Joel Tsevat, ""Religious Coping and Physiological, Psychological, Social, and Spiritual Outcomes in Patients with HIV/AIDS: Cross-Sectional and Longitudinal Findings", *AIDS and Behavior.* 14, no. 2 (2010): 379-389.

[156] Andrew P. Tix and Patricia F. Frazier, "The Use of Religious Coping During Stressful Life Events: Main Effects, Moderation, and Mediation," *Journal of Consulting and Clinical Psychology.* 66, no. 2 (1998): 411-422.

[157] Salvatore R. Maddi, Marnie Brwo, Doborah M. Khoshaba, and Mark Vaitkus, "Relationship of Hardiness and Religiousness to Depression and Anger," *Consulting Psychology Journal* 58, no. 3 (Summer 2006): 148-161.

[158] Viktor E. Frankl, "The Philosophical Foundations of Logotherapy." In Erwin W. Straus, *Phenomenology: Pure and Applied; The First Lexington Conference* (Pittsburgh: Duquesne University Press, 1964): 54.

the overlap of Frankl's notion of "will to meaning," and the meaning in life supplied by religion, spirituality and faith seems obvious and natural. Like the human tendency toward worship, the human search for meaning is, in Frankl's words, a "primary force" and not a secondary rationalization.[159] As Reuven P. Bulka observed when considering logotherapy's openness to, and accommodation of, Talmudic Judaism: "It is only a step from faith in ultimate meaning to faith in the architect of this ultimate meaning, faith in God."[160] After a careful reading of Frankl's work, Bulka concluded that when Frankl called logotherapy a secular theory and practice, he meant that logotherapy is *also* secular, that is, open to the secularist as well as the religious man. In other words, Bulka concluded that Frankl was compelled to maintain a certain parasecularity in order that logotherapy might be open to all, in part because the concepts in logotherapy border so closely on religious tenets.[161]

Still, the connection between the will to meaning, and the innate religious impulse, has not been lost on religious scholars. As Rabbi Abraham Joshua Heschel observed:

> Human being is never sheer being; it is always involved in meaning. The dimension of meaning is as indigenous to his being human as the dimension of space is to stars and stones.[162]

Herschel went on to explain that the concern for meaning is not self-imposed: it is a necessity of the human experience, so much so

---

[159] Frankl, *Will to Meaning*, 154.
[160] Reuven P. Bulka. "Logotherapy and Talmudic Judaism," *Journal of Religion and Health* 14, no. 4 (1975): 277.
[161] *Ibid*, pp. 277-278.
[162] Abraham Joshua Heschel. *Who Is Man?* (Stanford, CA: Stanford University Press, 1965): 51.

that each person is at any point in time either coming into meaning or betraying it.[163]

For their part, psychologists and social scientists have long recognized the significance of religious faith as a helpful and effective coping resource, even if the meaning and purpose that people find in their faith is not connected to, derived from, or associated with logotherapy or meaning therapy *per se*. It is understood that religion provides, in the terminology of social scientists, a "global meaning system."[164] When faced with stressful events, religious believers tend to reappraise their perceptions of such situations in light of their faith. This is understood by social scientists to be a process of "meaning-making coping."[165] And it works: meaning-seekers are often able to conclude their quest once they find meaning within a religious framework or through a spiritual practice.[166] Research has shown that once meaning has been made in association with faith (that is, once a stressful situation is resolved by reference to and integration with faith), distress is alleviated.[167]

The next chapter will show how this works within an evangelical Christian "global meaning system." The chapter will not include a comparison of religions or religious belief systems, but will focus

[163] *Ibid*, p. 54.
[164] *See* Crystal Park, "Religiousness/Spirituality and Health: A Meaning Systems Perspective," *Journal of Behavioral Medicine* 30, no. 4 (2007): 319-328.
[165] *See* Kenneth I. Pargament, Harold G. Koenig, and Lisa M. Perez. "The Many Methods of Religious Coping: Development and Initial Validation of the RCOPE." *Journal of Clinical Psychology* 56, no. 4 (2000): 519-43.
[166] LeRoy Gruner, "Heroin, Hashish, and Hallelujah: The Search for Meaning," *Review of Religious Research*. 26, no. 2 (1984): 176-186.
[167] *See* Roy F. Baumeister, *Meanings of Life* (New York: Guilford Press, 1991); and Ronnie Janoff-Bulman and Cynthia McPherson Frantz, "The Impact of Trauma on Meaning: From Meaningless World to Meaningful Life," in Michael J. Power and Chris Brewin, *The Transformation of Meaning in Psychological Therapies: Integrating Theory and Practice* (Chichester, England: Wiley, 1997): 91-107.

specifically on biblical Christianity. The premise of the next chapter is that a follower of Christ need not have training in logotherapy in order to appreciate the innate need for meaning in life on the part of every person, or to discuss a relationship with Jesus Christ in terms of meaningfulness and purposefulness.

4

DREAD AS EXISTENTIAL NEED FOR FAITH

One discovers God through confronting such questions as "Why" and "Who Am I?"

Prudence Allen[168]

Sisyphus and Futility

There is an ancient Greek myth – first attributed to Pherecydes – about a Corinthian king named Sisyphus.[169] Sisyphus, as the story is told, stole Aegina, daughter of Asopus, from Zeus while Zeus was carrying her through the Corinthian territory. In his anger, Zeus retaliated by sending Death against Sisyphus. However, Sisyphus also tricked both

---

[168] Prudence Allen, "Person and Complementarity in *Fides et Ratio*," in Foster, David Ruel, and Joseph W. Koterski, *The Two Wings of Catholic Thought: Essays on Fides et ratio* (Washington, D.C.: Catholic University of America Press, 2003): 39.

[169] Lowell Edmunds, *Approaches to Greek Myth* (Baltimore: Johns Hopkins University Press, 1990): 12.

Death and Hades, and ultimately managed to secure for himself a long life. After he died of old age, Hades condemned the dead Sisyphus to occupy himself forever by repeatedly rolling a stone up a mountain, only to see it roll back again into the valley.

Writers over the years have reacted to the story of Sisyphus with a variety of interpretations and observations. In the *Odyssey,* Homer's Hercules viewed Sisyphus with detached observation: the fact that Sisyphus was forever compelled to engage in his futile activity did not seem to strike Hercules as either good or bad. It just is.[170] Other writers have had a more visceral reaction to the story of Sisyphus. They recognize the futility of Sisyphus' labors as being a metaphor for life itself. Life, it would seem, is an essentially meaningless struggle (except in the case of Sisyphus) that is mercifully concluded with death.

Albert Camus's treatment of this story takes a different turn. For Camus, there is no inherent meaning to life. Worse, the meaninglessness of life's tasks can lead to misery. Camus acknowledges that the gods in the Greek pantheon believed "with some reason that there is no more dreadful punishment than futile and hopeless labor."[171] He acknowledges that the "workman of today works every day in his life at the same tasks, and his fate is no less absurd."[172]

And yet Camus argues that one must simply carry on. He declares that "There is no fate that cannot be surmounted by scorn,"[173] and that somehow the very fact that Sisyphus is "still on the go"[174] should serve

---

[170] Homer tells the story of Hercules' observation of Sisyphus during Hercules' visit to Hades while undertaking his twelfth labor, that is, his effort to catch and fetch Kerberos, the Hound of Hades. Richard P. Martin, *Myths of the Ancient Greeks* (New York: New American Library, 2003): 48-52.

[171] Albert Camus, *The Myth of Sisyphus and Other Essays*, trans, Justin O'Brien (New York: Vintage Books, 1955): 119.

[172] *Ibid*, p. 121.

[173] *Ibid.*

[174] *Ibid*, p. 123.

as a basis for his psychological escape from dread. Camus ends his essay with the following observation:

> I leave Sisyphus at the foot of the mountain! One always finds one's burden again. But Sisyphus teaches the higher fidelity that negates the gods and raises rocks. He too concludes that all is well. This universe henceforth without a master seems to him neither sterile nor futile. Each atom of that stone, each mineral flake of that night-filled mountain, in itself forms a world. The struggle itself toward the heights is enough to fill a man's heart. One must imagine Sisyphus happy.[175]

Qoheleth and Futility

According to the general narrative of the Judeo-Christian Bible, the universe is not without a Master. Nor is human life devoid of purpose. God is seated on His throne, and has sovereign authority over the nations (Psalm 47:8). God has a plan and a purpose for each human being (Jeremiah 29:11). In the overall Biblical regime, there is no place for existential or psychological dread because God is sovereign.

Of course, there never has been a universal worldwide acknowledgment of the sovereign God described in the Bible as being seated on his throne. Not everyone on earth recognizes this or has an appreciation for God's sovereignty. Indeed, the perspective of many people is somewhat horizontal, in the sense that it does not take into account the idea of a heavenly deity.

---

[175] *Ibid.*

All is Futility

The book of Ecclesiastes gives consideration to this horizontal perspective, often referred to within the writing as life "under the sun."[176] The writer of Ecclesiastes, known as Qoheleth ("the Preacher" or "the Teacher")[177] but generally understood to be King Solomon[178], had much to say about the futility and meaninglessness of life on this earth. He laments about the meaninglessness of life, o much so, that some authors have noticed that Ecclesiastes seems to reflect the same existential mood of futility that is woven through much of Camus' writings.[179] This mood, and this theme, is seen in the opening line where the Qoheleth writes off all of life as *hebel*, that is, as vanity, vapor, mist, airy nothing, or futility.

The thesis that life is essentially futile is set forth in the second verse of the book, Ecclesiastes 1:2: "Vanity of vanities, says the preacher, vanity of vanities! All is vanity." The argument for this claim is summarized

---

[176] The expression "under the sun" appears approximately twenty-six times in the Book of Ecclesiastes. A similar expression, "under heaven," appears three times, once each in the first three chapters of the book.

[177] The term "Ecclesiastes" comes from the Greek word *ekklēsiastēs* that translated the Hebrew *qohelet* ("one who speaks to the assembly"). Roger Norman Whybray, *Ecclesiastes* (Grand Rapids: Eerdmans, 1989): 2.

[178] The book is attributed at Ecclesiastes 1:1 to "the son of David, king in Jerusalem" and the speaker identifies himself as such: "I the Preacher have been king over Israel in Jerusalem." Ecclesiastes 1:12. However, many scholars doubt that the book was written directly by Solomon or transcribed during his lifetime. *See* Tremper Longman III, *The Book of Ecclesiastes* (Grand Rapids: Eerdmans, 1998): 4-8.

[179] *See*, e.g., Robert C. Solomon, *Dark Feelings, Grim Thoughts: Experience and Reflection in Camus and Sartre* (Oxford: Oxford University Press, 2006): 51. Solomon compares Camus' treatment of Sisyphus with the sense of futility and absurdity expressed in Ecclesiastes. *See also* Robert Asa, "The Faith of a Skeptic: The Enigma of Ecclesiastes," *Journal for the Liberal Arts and Sciences* 13, no. 3 (2009): 55-66. Asa observes that the writer of Ecclesiastes sounds more like Camus than Moses or Jesus. Ibid, 55.

in the next verse: "What does man gain by all the toil at which he toils under the sun?" Much of the rest of the first three chapters of the book of Ecclesiastes presents the case that under a horizontal perspective (where God is not necessarily taken into account), nothing can be done (i.e., no toil can be undertaken) that will ensure meaning and purpose in life.

The book begins at Ecclesiastes 1:2 with the declaration that "All is vanity!" and proceeds through a protracted essay on how nothing in this life ultimately provides meaning or true satisfaction. Not wealth,[180] or work,[181] or power,[182] or physical pleasures (food, sex, etc.)[183]. Not even wisdom itself fully satisfies.[184]

Qoheleth is not an atheist, but he makes many of his observations of life "under the sun," that is, from a horizontal view that does not necessarily presume divine intervention in the everyday activities of humans. In Ecclesiastes, he considers the limitations of human wisdom in a world where injustice,[185] the exigencies of life,[186] and death itself[187]

---

[180] Wealth does not satisfy according to Qoheleth. Ecclesiastes 4:7-8 and 5:9-6:9, and elsewhere in the text.

[181] Qoheleth concludes that to seek meaning in work proves ultimately to be futile endeavor. Ecclesiastes 2:18-23 and 4:4-6, and elsewhere in the text.

[182] Political power is ultimately meaningless. Ecclesiastes 4:13-16.

[183] The ultimate dissatisfaction of earthly pleasures is bemoaned at Ecclesiastes 2:1-11 and elsewhere in the book.

[184] Human wisdom and righteousness are better than folly, but are subject to inherent limitations (including limited human capacities, life's uncertainties, and death). Ecclesiastes 1:15-29; 8:16-17; 9:13-18 and elsewhere.

[185] Qoheleth expresses great concern about the unfairness of life. Ecclesiastes 3:16-22; 5:8-9; 8:10-15 and elsewhere.

[186] *E.g.*, Ecclesiastes 9:11-12 (time and chance affect everything); Ecclesiastes 10:5-11 (the accidents of life turn everything upside down); and Ecclesiastes 11:1-11 (there is risk and uncertainty at every turn in life).

[187] Death is the great leveler of life, rendering all of life so purposeless and so futile that it is worth asking if we are better off dead than alive (Ecclesiastes 4:1-3; 11:7-10).

serve to ultimately frustrate virtually all human endeavors. It is in Ecclesiastes that even the wisdom of Solomon as articulated so grandly in the biblical book of Proverbs is superior to foolishness and yet so inherently limited[188] that it becomes ultimately futile and pointless in view of death.[189]

The Futility of Wisdom, Pleasure, Living Well and Work

Five categories of such toils are presented by Qoheleth in the first three chapters of Ecclesiastes, and these categories are expanded upon later in the book. The first category is that of applied wisdom, with an emphasis on addressing societal problems. In Ecclesiastes 1:12-18, a passage clearly intended to remind us that the book of Ecclesiastes is drawn from, or points back to, the life and experience of Solomon, the author of Ecclesiastes claims to have searched out by wisdom all that is done under heaven. All of the wisdom in the world, it seems, cannot straighten out the problems of the world, and well-intended efforts to do so will only lead to frustration.

The second category of toils is that of self-indulgence, made possible by wealth and power. In Ecclesiastes 2:1-11, Qoheleth describes a lifestyle of expansive power and influence, which in turn made it possible for him to indulge himself lavishly in every possible pleasure. He advises that the effort it takes to build for himself such a lifestyle is essentially futile. Hedonism, it seems, is ultimately unsatisfying.

The third category of toils is that of living wisely. In Ecclesiastes 2:12-17 Qoheleth observes that at the end of the day the person who lives carefully and with reason and circumspection, dies. Even if that person's life is exemplary, there will come a time when even the memory of the wise person will likely fade. The wise person, like the

---

[188] *See* Ecclesiastes 7:15-22-29; 8:16-17; and 9:13-18.
[189] *Ibid.* Death renders both wisdom and folly meaningless (Ecclesiastes 2:1-11).

fool, will eventually die and will eventually be forgotten. Qoheleth, who obviously treasures wisdom, declares that this bitter reality causes him to hate life.

The fourth toil is that of work itself, described in Ecclesiastes 2:18-25. Even though there may be few things more rewarding than finding enjoyment in one's life work, everything that is accomplished will eventually be dissipated. Not only does the hard-working and productive person die, but any wealth or estate that he or she builds will be left behind to be enjoyed by someone who did not work for it. Looking back over one's life work, the end result will hardly have been worth the many long days and sleepless nights that characterized that work.

Eternity in the Heart

The fifth and perhaps most profound toil is the intractable struggle with time itself. Qoheleth highlights this phenomenon by writing a poem about time at Ecclesiastes 3:1-8, observing that "for everything there is a season and a time for every matter under heaven."After listing a series of alternating favorable and unfavorable tasks and life activities, e.g., planting and reaping, killing and healing, etc., Qoheleth asks, "What gain?"

This question points to the impossibility of timing everything in life correctly, and also to the reality that even if is timed as optimally as possible, all of life is sandwiched between the first two "matters:" birth and death. Embedded in this passage are layers of frustration: frustration that we can never catch up with our schedule of life's tasks; frustration that we can never figure out how to time our tasks optimally; and, most of all, frustration that time itself eventually runs out and makes all of life's tasks — whether they are timed well or not — futile in the long run.

It is at this point that Qoheleth points the reader to the greatest frustration of all, namely, the frustration that comes from the reality of life and death in light of the human expectation of and aspiration toward eternity. Qoheleth notes that even though all of life's experiences are positioned between birth and death, most people travel through life with at least some awareness of, and yearning for, the eternal. This, Qoheleth suggests at Ecclesiastes 3:11, is because God "has put eternity into man's heart." Indeed, none of the other toils would matter so much if the human experience were not characterized by a yearning for a meaning and a purpose that surpassed the delimiters of birth and death.

As with any translation of any passage in the Bible, there are sometimes differences in the interpretation of phrases or words. In the case of the expression "eternity in man's heart," the Hebrew word עולם translated into English as "eternity" (sometimes transliterated as *'owlam*) can have varying shades of meaning. In his well-researched article on this subject, Brian P. Gault concludes that the scholarly literature around עולם and its context yields as many as ten different interpretations. Of these, one or two of them clearly appear to be translation errors. But the rest of the possible ways in which to interpret עולם center around such notions as eternal work, perpetuity, awareness of remotest time, a desire to know the future, a desire for true permanence, and consciousness of the eternal.[190]

Compare: Temporality and Augustine's Restlessness

The "toil" or struggle to rise above the shackles of temporality and somehow connect with eternity is indeed common to the human experience. It has been considered at some length by various Christian

---

[190] Brian P. Gault, "A Reexamination of 'Eternity' in Ecclesiastes 3:11, *Biblotheca Sacra* 165 (January-March 2008): 39-57.

thinkers since the days of Qoheleth. Two of those thinkers, Augustine of Hippo and Blaise Pascal, will be briefly considered here.

As was mentioned in the introduction to this work, Augustine wrote that his heart was restless without God's peace. In the many volumes that comprise Augustine's body of work, he never articulates the precise nature of his pre-conversion restlessness. He does, however, highlight one particular concept that both troubled him and helped him to resolve his understanding of – and his faith in – God. That concept was the idea of time, especially the extent to which the human experience of time is itself bounded by birth and death. In this regard, Augustine shared with Qoheleth a profound appreciation for the significance – including the frustration – that death has on one's perspective of life.

Not long after his conversion to Christianity, Augustine took up the project of ascertaining what it meant to have happiness in this life. He concluded early in this investigation that a life that is not lived in complete surrender to God can never be a happy life. Indeed, the idea of a "happy life without God" is to some extent an oxymoron.

The human experience is to a large extent a life marked by unmet expectations, unfulfilled dreams, and disappointments. In part, this is because the experience of life is inevitably accompanied by the experience of death.

Augustine's *Confessions*, written in the latter part of his life, took into account his memory of his initial conversion. As part of his story, Augustine recalls the sorrow and misery that he experienced after the death of a dear friend. He sought consolation from many sources and quarters, but found them wanting:

> Feverishly I thrashed about, sighed, wept and was troubled, and there was no repose for me, nor any counsel. Within me I was carrying a tattered, bleeding

soul that did not want me to carry it, yet I could find no place to lay it down. Not in pleasant countryside did it find rest, nor in shows and songs, nor in sweet-scented gardens, nor in elaborate feasts, nor in the pleasures of couch or bed, nor even in books and incantations.[191]

Along the way, as part of this grieving process, Augustine became acutely aware of the temporality of life. He observed the essential conflict between the human experience of the cycles of life and death, and a deeper desire for things eternal:

[F]or wheresoever a human soul turns, it can but cling to what brings sorrow unless it turns to you, playing though it may to beautiful things outside you and outside itself. Yet were these beautiful things and not from you, none of them would be at all. They are rise and sink; in their rising they begin to exist and grow toward their perfection, but once perfect they grow old and parish; or, if not all reach old age, yet certainly all parish. So then, even as they arise and stretch out toward existence, the more quickly they grow and strive to be, the more swiftly they are hastening toward extinction.[192]

Temporality, and awareness of temporality, is for Augustine a key cause of restlessness in the human spirit. So much so that he devoted an entire book of his thirteen-book *Confessions* to a consideration of the difference between the time-bound human experience, and the timeless and eternal nature of God the Creator of time. The first ten

---

[191] Augustine, *Confessions* § 4.7.12, 61.
[192] Augustine, *Confessions* § 4.10.15, 63.

books of his *Confessions* are biographical, in that they explore and explain the circumstances and the impact of Augustine's conversion. The last two books, that is, the twelfth and thirteenth, address God and His creation, and serve as a commentary on the first chapter of the biblical book of Genesis. Book Eleven of Augustine's *Confessions* serves as his exploration of time and eternity. Richard Avramenko explains this arrangement as follows:

> [T]o be happy, we must know ourselves (hence the first ten books); but knowing ourselves is wholly contingent upon knowing God and His creation (hence the last two books). Consequently, what lies between man and God is a book on time. Time, therefore, separates man from God, yet paradoxically it is also the nexus between man and God. To know God, one must know time.[193]

Avramenko refers to the "wounding" of time because any inquiry into time necessitates some consideration of what lies outside its parameters: "In Augustine's ontology, one cannot inquire into the nature of time without inquiring into eternity; time makes no sense unless it stands in contradistinction to eternity."[194]

Furthermore, eternity is inextricably bound up with God, who exists outside of time. The more we become aware of the gulf between time and eternity, the more we are forced to acknowledge the gap between man and God. The separation between time and eternity parallels this gap and teaches us about this gap. As a result, "the human-divine unity required for true happiness becomes all but impossible."[195]

---

[193] Richard Avramenko-, "The Wound and Salve of Time: Augustine's Politics of Human Happiness," *The Review of Metaphysics* no. 60 (June 2007): 782.

[194] *Ibid*, p. 783.

[195] Ibid, 783.

This helps to explain the restlessness of which Augustine spoke at the outset of his *Confessions*.

Compare: Pascal's "Knowledge of the Heart"

This essential tension between finitude and infinity was also acknowledged by Blaise Pascal. Pascal's unfinished work, *Pensees*, serves as a collection of his thoughts and ideas about man, God, and the Christian experience. Like Qoheleth and Augustine, Pascal understood the human experience to be one of uneasiness, anxiety and ambivalence, caused at least in part by the awareness of eternity. Life, for Pascal, is constant movement, only to be truncated by death.[196] He wrote that the eternity "of things in themselves or in God must always astonish our brief duration."[197] Eternity, in fact, is not only astonishing, but also frightening:

> When I consider the brief duration of my life absorbed in the eternity that lies before and after – the memory of a guest who stays only a day – the small space I occupy and can even see, engulfed in the infinite immensity of spaces I do not know and that do not know me, I am frightened and astonished to see myself here rather than there; for there is no reason why I am here rather than there, why now rather than then. Who put me here? By whose order and direction have this place and time been allotted to me?[198]

---

[196] Pascal and Ariew, *Pensées* S230/L199/B72, 63.
[197] *Ibid*, S529/L641/B129, 166 ("Our nature consists in motion; complete rest is death.").
[198] *Ibid*, S102/L68/B205, 22.

Indeed, the very thought of considering human mortality in light of a larger awareness of eternity can be, for Pascal, terrifying:

> I see those terrifying spaces of the universe that surround me, and I find myself tied to one corner of this vast expanse, without knowing why I am put in this place rather than in another, nor why the short time given me to live is assigned to me at this point rather than at another of the whole eternity that preceded me or the one that will follow me. · I see nothing but infinites on all sides, surrounding me like an atom and like a shadow that lasts only for an instant and returns no more.[199]

As Blaise Pascal looked around, he noticed that in his experience not everyone appeared to be astonished, frightened, or terrified by the idea of eternity. He found this to be very troubling. He could not understand it, and considered it to be puzzling and "unnatural":

> Nothing is so important to man as his own state; nothing is so terrifying to him as eternity. And thus it is not natural that there should be men indifferent to the loss of their existence and to the peril of an eternity of wretchedness. They behave quite differently with regard to all other things: they fear even the slightest ones, foresee them, feel them. And this same man who spends so many days and nights in rage and despair at the loss of some office, or because of an imaginary insult to his honor, is the very one who knows, without anxiety and without emotion, that he

---

[199] *Ibid*, S681/L427/B194, 218.

will lose everything through death. It is a monstrous thing to see in the same heart and at the same time this sensitivity to the slightest things and this strange insensitivity to the greatest.[200]

Pascal was concerned about people who chose to ignore the implications of eternity. He considered them to be unreasonable, if not outright foolish. They were, in today's parlance, living in a state of denial:

There is nothing clearer than this, and so, according to the principles of reason, men's behavior is wholly unreasonable if they do not take another path. Let us, therefore, on this point judge those who live without thinking of the ultimate end of life, who let themselves be guided by their inclinations and their pleasures without reflection and without concern, as if they could annihilate eternity by turning their thought away from it, and think only of making themselves happy for the moment. Yet this eternity exists, and death, which must begin it and which threatens them every hour, must in a short time inevitably put them under the horrible necessity of being annihilated or unhappy eternally, without their knowing which of these eternities has been prepared for them forever.[201]

Pascal concluded that this state of denial leads people to find amusements and diversions in order to dull their awareness of things eternal. He declared that people are so vain and empty that even

---

[200] *Ibid,* S681/L427/B194, 219.
[201] *Ibid,* S681/L427/B194, 221.

though they have a thousand reasons for boredom, the least thing such as pushing a billiard ball with a cue is enough to amuse them.[202] He summed up the human experience as constituting a desperate attempt to avoid solitude and self-assessment. In a manner similar to Qoheleth's acknowledgment that pleasure never satisfies,[203] Pascal showcases the most privileged position of his time – i.e., that of a king – as the ultimate case study for the human need for such diversion:

> However, let us imagine a king with all the advantages pertaining to his rank. If he is without diversion, left to ponder and reflect on what he is, this languishing felicity will not sustain him. He will necessarily come to think about the threats facing him, revolts that may occur, and, in the end, inevitable death and disease. As a result, if he is without what is called diversion, he is unhappy, even unhappier than the least of his subjects playing and diverting himself.[204]

Not that Pascal considered the human impulse and effort to avoid coming to grips with the finitude/infinity dilemma as being wise. He did not. In fact, his well known "Wager" is presented in the *Pensées* as an example of the foolishness of most people. To the extent that God is eternal, and to the extent that the utilities or benefits of seeking God and believing in him on His terms are infinite, people make a bad bet when they ignore the eternal in favor -of the temporal.

Pascal saw the human tendency to try to find permanent satisfaction with less-than-infinite (temporal) distractions and diversions as great

---

[202] *Ibid*, S168/L136/B139, 40.

[203] E.g. at Ecclesiastes 2:1-11, summarized at verse 11b: "... and behold, all was vanity and a striving after wind, and there was nothing to be gained under the sun."

[204] Pascal and Ariew, *Pensées* S168/L136/B139, 39.

foolishness.[205] He reasoned that people make this choice in order to avoid the reality of their desperate state:

> Were we to relieve them of all these cares, they would then see themselves and think about what they are, where they came from, where they are going. So, it is not possible to occupy and divert them too much. This is why, after we have set up so many duties for them, if they have any time for relaxation, we advise them to use it on diversion and play and always to keep fully occupied.[206]

In view of this willfulness toward absolute folly, Pascal drew a simple and succinct conclusion: "How hollow and full of garbage is the heart of man."[207]

Atheism and Futility

Augustine and Pascal were not atheists, and they drew very clear distinctions between the perspective of believers and nonbelievers. Nor was Ecclesiastes written by an atheist. Qoheleth also carefully differentiates between the horizontal view of life "under the sun" and a vertical view of life that takes into account the presence of God. He

---

[205] A full discussion of Pascal's Wager is beyond the scope of this work. There is, however, a rich literature on this topic. Two of the more recent contributions to the scholarship on the subject of Pascal's Wager include: Bradley Monton, "Mixed Strategies Can't Evade Pascal's Wager," *Analysis* 71, no. 4 (2011): 642-645; and Daniel Garber, *What Happens After Pascal's Wager: Living Faith and Rational Belief* (Milwaukee, WI: Marquette University Press, 2009). The latter work is reviewed at: Elizabeth Burns, "What Happens After Pascal's Wager: Living Faith and Rational Belief - Daniel Garber," *The Philosophical Quarterly* 61, no. 242 (2011): 218-221.
[206] Pascal and Ariew, *Pensées* S171/L139/B143, 43.
[207] *Ibid.*

never denies that God is above the sun, or that God may indeed have His own perspective of the earth and its inhabitants. In a sense, the entire book of Ecclesiastes seems to be a prayer, asking God to reveal His meaning for our existence.

If the existence of God is denied, on the other hand, everything changes. Historically, this is what happened when Friedrich Nietzsche declared the death of God. The theistic grand narrative of Judeo-Christianity upon which the Bible is based, and which largely informed Western thinking until the late 19th century, was declared dead in Nietzsche's parable of the madman who cried: "Whither is God? I will tell you. We have killed him-you and I. All of us are his murderers. God is dead. God remains dead. And we have killed him."[208]

Nietzsche's declaration signified a new sense of meaninglessness in the absence of a sovereign Creator. By comparison, Qoheleth's sense of futility of life under the sun had still left open the possibility that a Creator-God – who reigned from above the sun – was to be considered and respected and feared, and was One from whom meaning could ultimately be derived. Nietzsche, however, set aside any such possibility of theistic and objective meaning. The futility and meaninglessness as articulated by Qoheleth was exacerbated and made more comprehensive by Nietzsche's negation of the possibility of oversight by God.

Without God, and without an external, objective reference point in the quest for meaning, the human experience is characterized by at least some level of anxiety. Martin Heidegger described this anxiety in terms of our being "thrown into existence" without a plan and without any direction.[209] As Heidegger understood the plight of mankind,

---

[208] Friedrich Nietzsche, *The Gay Science*, ed. Bernard Williams, trans. Josefine Nauckhoff and Adrian Del Caro (New York: Cambridge University Press, 2001): § 125.

[209] Martin Heidegger, *Being and Time.* trans. John Macquarrie and Edward Robinson. (New York: Harper and Row, 1962): 276H.

each individual human is alone in this "thrownness" and therefore experiences dread as a result of such solitude in the midst of a void.

The Existential Need for Faith

Binary Oppositions: Emotion versus Reason

Modernism has been characterized by the "binary oppositions of the Enlightenment epistemology" such as the tension between reason and faith.[210] In the introduction to his book *Existential Reasons for Belief in God: A Defense of Desires and Emotions for Faith*, Clifford Williams observes that traditional Protestant and Catholic Christianity has also been characterized by such binary oppositions. One of those binary oppositions is the tension between the role that the satisfaction of needs should play, as compared to the role that reason should play, in acquiring and sustaining faith. Another binary opposition is that of the tension between faith understood as the acceptance of certain biblical truth-claims, and faith understood as truly a change of heart that encompasses emotional depth.[211]

Williams suggests that there tends to be some overlapping of these two dichotomies. "Head"-oriented Christians think of faith mostly in terms of faith as assent-through-reason, while "heart"-oriented Christians think of faith at least to some extent as commitment-with-emotional-needs-satisfaction.[212] Although he does not attempt to gather or point to any empirical data regarding the extent to which Christian populations drift in either direction, Williams

---

[210] George Lindbeck, "Forward" In *By the Renewing of Your Minds: The Pastoral Function of Christian Doctrine,* edited by Ellen T. Charry (New York: Oxford University Press, 1997): xiii-xiv.

[211] Clifford Williams, *Existential Reasons for Belief in God: A Defense of Desires and Emotions for Faith* (Downers Grove, IL: IVP Academic, 2011):11-12.

[212] *Ibid.*

takes on the project of asking whether there is any legitimacy to the acquisition of faith in God solely through the satisfaction of needs, and also asking whether faith in God consists, at least in part, -in emotions. Many Christians might object to any emphasis on emotions and heart orientation. In most cases, those very same Christians find themselves worshiping through music and song on Sunday mornings, not solely listening to sermons and Bible instruction.

As part of his attempt to find a middle ground between emotion and need, on the one hand, and reasoned assent on the other, Williams finds himself making the case for the acquisition of faith through need, emotion and reason. He proposes that satisfaction of need is a legitimate and appropriate dynamic that can draw people to faith, so long as reason is involved in the process. In fact, he considers emotion and need to be as trustworthy for faith in God as reason. The author acknowledges that emotions (like reason) can lead one astray, but that the development and embracing of the right emotions rather than the suppression of emotions altogether ought to be pursued as a primary solution. In the same manner, bad reasoning can lead one astray, and the solution to this problem is the development of better reasoning skills, not the abandonment of reason.[213]

Existential Neediness

When the term "emotion" is juxtaposed against reason, cognition or rationality, it requires some explanation. In this context, emotion is often a vague concept that can include a variety of psychological, emotional and even spiritual impulses or passions. For purposes of this discussion about non-rational needs that may be met by religious faith, Williams adopts the term "existential needs." These include, among others, felt needs for: (a) cosmic security, or the assurance that all will

---

[213] *Ibid.*

not be lost despite possible hardships or disasters; (b) the assurance that consciousness will not end at death; (c) a larger life, that is a desire for a more expansive life that will include new experiences and possible improvements to one's current existence; (d) meaning, defined primarily in terms of a life of love; and (e) forgiveness for having gone astray and having made oneself unlovable.[214]

In some ways Williams' taxonomy describes the human experience as an effort to stay within a corridor of contentment that seeks something more in life while desperately grasping to avoid losing that which we already have. This "something more in life" cannot be satisfied, Williams suggests, with anything other than faith. For some people, it is obvious that faith in something supernatural is the only thing that would work. Other people may try non-faith means of fulfilling this need for something more in life, but will usually find those means and those efforts to be relatively frivolous and unsatisfying.[215]

Of these various needs listed above, the need for cosmic security seems to be the most dominant and the most comprehensive. Williams articulates this need in a way that takes into account many of the other needs, as follows:

> We need to know that we will live beyond the grave in a state that is free from the defects of this life, a state that is full of goodness and justice. We need a more expansive life, one in which we love and are loved. We need meaning, and we need to know that we are forgiven for going astray. We also need to experience, to delight in goodness and to be present with those we love.[216]

---

[214] *Ibid*, pp. 21-24.
[215] *Ibid*, p. 36.
[216] *Ibid*, p. 32.

Williams refers to these needs as "existential" in part because they correspond to the kinds of spiritual, psychological and emotional needs that were articulated by Søren Kierkegaard, one of the earliest existentialists. Indeed, Williams points his readers to Kierkegaard's commentary on Matthew 11:28,[217] "Come to me, all who labor and are heavy laden, and I will give you rest."[218] In that commentary, Kierkegaard declares that Christ's invitation extends to everyone in every circumstance who has any sense of profound need. This includes those who are poor and wretched, who must slave away their lives in poverty to secure for themselves a meager existence; those who are suffering from miserable diseases (such as leprosy) and who are bedridden; those who are so sick at heart that they question whether there is a difference between human and animal suffering; those who are so depressed that for them only "death distinguishes death from life;" those who labor in futility; and those who are under the bondage of sin, "where the way of sin turns more deeply into sin."[219]

Williams argues that these needs justify belief in God. His argument is simple: God satisfies the human need for cosmic security; therefore, having faith in God is justified.[220] Each person has a need to believe in God in order to avoid constant anguish about cosmic security, life beyond the grave and what a good life involves. Not unlike the husband who needs to believe that his wife is faithful if he is to avoid maltreating her, even though that need does not lead him to hire a detective to follow his wife's movements. Similarly, a mother has a need to believe that her son is alive, so that she does not go to pieces

---

[217] *Ibid*, p. 33, n.1, referring to Søren Kierkegaard, *The Practice of Christianity*, trans. Howard V. Hong and Edna H. Hong (Princeton: Princeton University Press, 1991): 16-20.

[218] All Bible quotations are from the English Standard Version (ESV) unless otherwise indicated.

[219] Kierkegaard, *Practice of Christianity*, 16-20.

[220] *Ibid*, p. 32.

psychologically. Likewise, a lawyer may need to believe that his client is innocent if he is to make a good speech in his defense. [221]

Reason as a Necessary but Insufficient Basis for Faith

Faith requires the intellectual understanding of, and assent to, truth-claims, and so faith without any reason (including emotional responses to religious experiences) is a non sequitur. What is less obvious, however, is whether faith based on reason alone makes sense. It made sense, at least to a large extent, to Aquinas as he formulated his five cosmological arguments for the existence of God. It also made sense to 18th century philosopher-theologians such as Leibniz and Samuel Clarke and their progeny. But the reason-based approach to natural theology was also roundly countered by philosophers from David Hume to Bertrand Russell, who have presented solid, if not entirely persuasive, rebuttals to the notion that faith is rational.

For our purposes here, though, as we ask whether reason is a necessary but insufficient basis for faith, we are starting with the presumption that faith is at least reasonable. After all, reason itself can be used to show that faith is reasonable. Reason helps us to understand that God exists, and helps us to understand what God is like. In fact, the Bible asserts that each person is accountable for his or her understanding that God exists and in response to that general revelation, is accountable for his or her understanding of what God is like:

> For the wrath of God is revealed from heaven against all ungodliness and unrighteousness of men, who by their unrighteousness suppress the truth. For what can be known about God is plain to them, because

---

[221] *Ibid*, pp. 45-46.

God has shown it to them. For his invisible attributes,
namely, his eternal power and divine nature, have been
clearly perceived, ever since the creation of the world,
in the things that have been made. So they are without
excuse. (Romans 1:18-20)

Possible barriers to faith, such as questions about the existence of
God, the historical reality of the incarnation and the resurrection, the
problem of evil, and similar issues, are routinely addressed by Christian
apologists, who, in turn, are called upon to always be prepared to make
a defense to anyone who asks for a reason for their hope in life (1 Peter
3:15). Reasoning also helps nonbelievers understand the basic precepts
of the gospel, as well as some of the more subtle doctrines, such as the
doctrine of the Trinity.[222]

Reason by itself however, is not equal to faith. As it is understood in
the Christian tradition, Christian faith is more than assent to a specific
set of truth-claims. It is, in a word, a relationship. A relationship that
involves faith in God, love of God, and trust in God.

Faith, then, requires reason plus something else. Faith engages the
whole person, and includes intellectual, volitional and emotional assent
as well as spiritual regeneration. The intellectual component of faith
takes into account reason and the wholehearted acceptance of truth-
claims. The volitional component involves the will and the intentional
decision to become, in the case of the Christian faith, a follower of Jesus
Christ. The spiritual component involves the work of the Holy Spirit
in regenerating the heart of the new believer.

It is the emotional component of faith, i.e., the aspect of faith that

---

[222] The reasonableness of faith is an age-old question with which apologists and
theologians have been wrestling for centuries. There are many resources available
for those who would care to look into this question more deeply, not the least of
which is Alvin Plantinga, *Warranted Christian Belief* (New York: Oxford University
Press, 2000).

engenders feelings of assurance, trust and confidence in Jesus Christ – so much so that He becomes the object of worship – that seems to cause some confusion. Indeed, Williams sets forth a number of critiques that have been leveled against emotion, such as the essential instability of emotions, their intense but short-term nature, the disruptive role that emotions can play in the life of a "rational" person, the fact that emotions are often unplanned and not rationally initiated or controlled, and the fact that emotions are not necessarily grounded in reason.[223]

Williams addresses each of these concerns about the role of emotion in faith, for the most part by showing that there is an appropriate and necessary middle ground between dry, rationalized acceptance of truth-claims, on the one hand, and mindless or blind religious experience on the other. More importantly, Williams reminds his readers that a true understanding of emotion involves an appreciation for the fact that emotions themselves consist partially of reason. That is, emotion, properly understood, is tied to reason, just as faith is tied to reason. And so for faith to be genuine, it should consist, at least partly, of emotions. His thesis in this regard is summed up as follows: "Because faith in God consists partly of satisfaction of need, and because satisfaction of need is an emotion, faith in God consists partly of emotions."[224]

Ignoring or Suppressing the Existential Need for Faith

Secular Theories about Religious Impulse

The idea that faith satisfies a need is not unique to Williams, nor is it unique to the human experience generally. Of the approximately 6.8 million people in the world, for example, it is estimated that somewhere between 84% and 90% are religious believers or adherents

---

[223] Williams, *Existential Reasons*, pp. 152-160.
[224] *Ibid*, p. 152.

of some sort.[225] Despite the influence of modernism in Western and other cultures (and the attendant predictions that modernism would necessarily usher in worldwide secularism[226]), the religious impulse is alive and well today.

It can be interesting, if not amusing, to hear non-religious (and anti-religious) "experts" attempt to explain this human impulse toward religion. In his classic tome on the psychology of religion, Geoffrey E. W. Scobie summarizes various theories of religion offered by modern psychologists and sociologists.[227] These include Sigmund Freud, who proposed a "frustration theory" premised on the notion that religion is one way of compensating for or adapting to the many frustrations of society and life in general. Another theory put forward by psychoanalysts has been the "conflict theory", which treats religion as a means of relieving guilt feelings experienced by people who blame themselves for various shortcomings and wrongdoings. A third explanation, known as "cognitive needs theory," suggests that the human desire to understand or give meaning to the universe and to their own personal life prompts people in the direction of religious faith. Another is the "social support hypothesis",which emphasizes the tendency of people to join groups that have beliefs similar to their own.[228]

---

[225] David B. Barrett, George T. Kurian and Todd M. Mohnson, *World Christian Encyclopedia*, vol. 1 (New York: Oxford University Press, 2001): 3. *See also* Adherents. com, "Major Religions of the World Ranked by Number of Adherents," http:// adherents.com/Religions_by_Adherents.html (accessed at February 3, 2012).

[226] *See* Rodney Stark and Roger Finke, *Acts of Faith: Explaining the Human Side of Religion* (Berkely: University of Califorinia Press, 2000): 57, quoting Thomas Jefferson as having stated in 1882: "There is not a young man now living in the United States who will not die a Unitarian." *See also* Rodney Stark, "Secularization, R.I.P." *Sociology of Religion* 60, no. 3 (October 1, 1999): 249-273, asserting at p. 251 that "there is universal agreement that modernism is the causal engine dragging the gods into retirement."

[227] Geoffrey E. W. Scobie, *Psychology of Religion* (New York: Wiley, 1975).

[228] *Ibid*, pp. 97-101.

All of these theories, and others, represent attempts by social scientists to explain the religious impulse. However well-founded, helpful or insightful they might or might not be, they all have as a common premise the acknowledgment that religious impulse is a common characteristic of the human experience. And so for most people, the question of faith is not whether or not to believe, or to worship, or to seek God. The question is how to do so.

The Dissatisfaction of Atheism

Many atheists acknowledge a certain amount of dissonance, dissatisfaction, and even despair because their rational commitment to atheism does not provide emotional or psychological resolution for them. Intellectual satisfaction about atheism does not equate to emotional and psychological contentment.

Woody Allen serves as an example of this tension between atheism and human emotional and psychological needs. In an article entitled "Religion, God and the Meaninglessness of it all in Woody Allen's Thought and Films," Johanna Petsche makes the following observation about the actor, author and film director:

> In his films dating from 1975 to 1989 Woody Allen rigorously explores themes of religion, God, morality and death as he compulsively examines and questions his atheistic outlook. At the core of these films lies Allen's existential dilemma in which his intellectual tendency towards atheism conflicts with his emotional need for meaning, objective moral values and justice,

all of which he strongly associates with the existence of God.[229]

In her review of Woody Allen's films, Petsche makes the case that many of these works offer a consistent and artistic expression of this conflict between his emotional need for meaning and his intellectual atheism.[230]

Conclusion

From Qoheleth to Camus, and in the writings of many other thinkers and philosophers, the notion of "futility" is often found and often emphasized. Life is futile. Work is futile. Pleasure is fleeting and futile. Just about every effort to find and identify that which really matters results in a common conclusion: nothing really matters.

Underlying the concern about futility, however, is frustration. The inference drawn by the reader of many of these writers is that the reader ought to be able to recognize the obvious futility of life. The reader then must deal with the accompanying frustration in some way. That is, the reader either needs to simply accept the futility of life and somehow let go of the accompanying or resulting frustration, or, the reader needs to respond to the frustration by continuing to pursue purpose in life.

The intellectual histories of philosophy, psychology and religion reflect an unwillingness on the part of many thinkers to ignore their frustration about the apparent meaninglessness of life. They continue to

---

[229] Johanna Petsche, "Religion, God and the Meaninglessness of it all in Woody Allen's Thought and Films," *Sydney Studies in Religion*, 2009, http://escholarship. usyd.edu.au/journals/index.php/SSR/article/view/712 (accessed at January 27, 2012).

[230] *Ibid.*

pursue, to think, to write and to express in their writings their ongoing efforts to wrestle with this existential and intellectual irritation.

At the same time, one "solution" to the problem is often proffered. That solution is faith. Qoheleth, for example, concludes his essay on the futility of life with the following punchline at Ecclesiastes 12:13: "The end of the matter; all has been heard. Fear God and keep his commandments, for this is the whole duty of man." Here is a very loose paraphrase: "Set aside your obsession with futility, acknowledge God for who He is, and place yourself in His program and purpose rather than your own." Eternity is hard-wired into the heart, causing a frustration about the meaning in life ... a frustration that can only be fully set aside when it is replaced by faith.

Augustine's thesis carries with it the same theme. Augustine "blames" God for creating us with a built-in desire for something larger than this life. And that something can only be found in the Creator Himself:

> You arouse us so that praising you may bring us joy,
> because you have made us and drawn us to yourself,
> and our heart is unquiet until it rests in you.[231]

Pascal echoes both Qoheleth and Augustine by asking, "If man is not made for God, why is he happy only in God?"[232] In fact, Pascal responds to the human propensity to seek meaning and contentment in life by offering the following advice:

> Do not look for satisfaction on earth; do not hope for
> anything from humans. Your good is only in God, and
> supreme felicity lies in knowing God, in being united

---

[231] Augustine and Boulding, *Confessions*, 3.
[232] Pascal and Ariew, *Pensées* S18/L399/B438, 4.

to him forever in eternity. Your duty is to love him with all your heart. He created you.[233]

For Kierkegaard, there is no match for the contentment that is derived from faith:

I can well endure living in my own fashion, I am happy and content, but my joy is not that of faith and in comparison with that is really unhappy.[234]

Like Augustine, Kierkegaard understood faith as an experience of rest in the wake of the turmoil of meaning-seeking. "Faith," Kierkegaard observed, "is that the self in being itself and willing to be itself rests transparently in God."[235]

de Unamuno defines faith as follows:

For faith is not the mere adherence of the intellect to an abstract principle, it is not the recognition of a theoretical truth, a process wherein the will merely moves us to believe; faith is an act of the will, it is a movement of the spirit toward a practical truth, toward a person, toward something which makes us not merely understand life but also makes us live it.[236]

---

[233] *Ibid*, S182/L149/B430, 47.

[234] Søren Kierkegaard. *Fear and Trembling*, ed. C. Stephen Evans, and Sylvia Walsh (Cambridge: Cambridge University Press, 2006): 28.

[235] Søren Kierkegaard, *The Sickness unto Death: A Christian Psychological Exposition for Upbuilding and Awakening* ed. and trans. Howard V. Hong, and Edna H. Hong (Princeton, N.J.: Princeton University Press, 1980): 82.

[236] Miguel de Unamuno, *Tragic Sense of Life in Men and Nations*, ed. Nartin Nozick, trans. Anthony Kerrigan (Princeton, NJ: Princeton University Press, 1978):210.

Faith for de Unamuno is so essential to life that there is an insatiable restlessness experienced by the faithless. He observes:

> I cannot believe that anyone who has once, either in his youth or some other period, harbored a faith in the immortality of the soul will ever be able to rest easy without that faith.[237]

Taken together, this chorus of writers and thinkers affirms Clifford Williams' thesis that there is within the human experience an existential need for God.

---

[237] de Unamuno and Kerrigan, *Tragic Sense of Life*, p. 113.

5

DREAD AS GRACE

For when dreams increase and words grow many, there is vanity; but God is the one you must fear.

Ecclesiastes 5:7

Faith and Doubt

"Some Doubted"

Matthew 28 is one of the most amazing chapters in the New Testament. It opens with a dramatic description of the resurrection of Christ, complete with an earthquake, guards frightened nearly to death, and the appearance of Christ that was described as being like lightning. Twice in the chapter disciples are so dazzled by the appearance of the resurrected Jesus that they worship him. The chapter ends with the Great Commission, wherein Jesus directs his disciples to bring His message of good news to the entire world.

Buried in this dramatic passage are two words that can seem to be strange and out of place. Those two words at Matthew 28:17 are, "some doubted." Despite an entire history of fulfilled prophecy represented by the person of the risen Christ, despite the various events leading to and surrounding the resurrection itself, and despite the undeniable reality of the appearance of Jesus Christ in their midst, some among the disciples doubted. Their five senses, and their ability to reason and induce, did not lead them to the same conclusion arrived at by many others who were faced with the same evidence of the resurrection.

There can be different explanations for the disparate reactions of people at the time of the resurrection of Jesus Christ. Some who doubted may have been persuaded by the "rebuttal evidence" in the form of rumors that the body of Jesus Christ had been stolen, such rumors having been planted by the chief priests (Matthew 28:11-15). Others may not have believed their own eyes, concluding that they were seeing a ghost or some other apparition rather than the same Jesus Christ who had been crucified and buried. Still others may have concluded, as did Thomas (John 20:24-25), that they did not have sufficient evidence in order to believe at some level (e.g., a preponderance of the evidence, clear and convincing evidence, or evidence that removed reasonable doubt).

There will Always be Some who Doubt

It was not unusual for people who came face-to-face with Jesus Christ to disbelieve or doubt. From time to time, he challenged their lack of faith while teaching about God's sovereignty and faithfulness, such as at Matthew 6:25-34 when He spoke about the birds of the air and the lilies of the field. His disciples, including and in particular Peter, were doubters from time to time (Matthew 14:28-3; 16:8-12; and 17:14-21).

The Bible demonstrates Biblical doubt in the face of compelling evidence at several points in its narrative. Moses doubted God, even as God performed miracles such as turning his staff into a snake and causing leprosy to appear and disappear on Moses' hand (Exodus 4). Abraham's story involving Sara is a series of episodes showing his lack of faith in God as well as a lack of faithfulness toward her (Genesis 12). Despite God's display of His power and sovereignty, doubt prevailed from time to time.

The Bible does not hold out the notion that faith is or can be compelled by reason. Certainly there is evidence from the natural world that serves as general revelation of a creator, but the acceptance of the truth claim that God is the Creator is a choice that is made by each individual in the face of such evidence. Choosing not to believe renders a person culpable (Romans 1:20). There is no escape from such culpability simply because supernatural miracles are not exhibited personally to each person (Luke 16:31). Instead, those who believe without benefit of signs and wonders are commended (John 20:29).

Cornelius Van Til proposed a way of thinking about the will-to-believe (or conversely the will-to-disbelieve) by considering the presuppositions that people bring to their analysis of a truth-claim. But apologists other than presuppositionalists, such as evidentialists, are more open to the notion that general revelation, history and miracles provide evidence for God that is accessible by nonbelievers, but do not insist that such nonbelievers are compelled to arrive at specific conclusions about God when faced with such evidence. Instead, apologists of all stripes understand that despite even overwhelming evidence, people generally reserve to themselves the freedom and the choice to believe or not believe. Their choice to disbelieve a proposition despite even compelling evidence does not necessarily render them non-rational.

Choosing to Believe, or Not

The idea of will-to believe (and will-to-disbelieve) in the face of, or despite, compelling evidence is not confined to Christian theology or philosophy. Within philosophical circles generally, belief is not dependent solely upon evidence or reason. No matter how solid the evidence for a truth-claim might be, and no matter how solidly warranted that claim might be, some people will from time to time reject the claim.

The problem of the seemingly irrational rejection of properly supported and properly warranted truth-claims is a broad subject that has been separately addressed outside of this work.[238] For purposes of this work, it is sufficient to observe that belief is not necessitated, dictated or required by logic or rationality. Belief in a truth-claim may be epistemologically unjustified under a scientific model if one does not have at least some evidence for it, but this premise is not necessitated metaphysically.

To at least some extent, people choose what to believe, and those choices reflect a certain willfulness or intentionality. Why? Some, like William James, argue that self-interest appears to have a role. In his essay *Will to Believe,* he acknowledged that for many decisions, the ultimate influence informing our choice is "passional," that is, not necessarily governed by rationality. "When we look at certain facts," he observed, "it seems as if our passional and volitional nature are at the root of all our convictions."[239] He expands on this concept as follows:

---

[238] *See, e.g.* Edward Stein, *Without Good Reason: The Rationality Debate in Philosophy and Cognitive Science* (Oxford: Clarendon Press, 1996).

[239] William James, *The Will to Believe: And Other Essays in Popular Philosophy, Human Immortality; Two Supposed Objections to the Doctrine* (New York: Dover, 1956): 117.

Evidently, then, our non-intellectual nature does influence our convictions. There are passional tendencies and volitions which run before and others which come after belief, and it is only the latter that are too late for the fair; and they are not too late when the previous passional work has been already in their own direction... Our passional nature not only lawfully may, but must, decide an option between propositions, whenever it is a genuine option that cannot by its nature be decided on intellectual grounds; for to say, under such circumstances, "Do not decide, but leave the question open," is itself a passional decision,–just like deciding yes or no,–and is attended with the same risk of losing the truth.[240]

Our sense of rationality, in turn, is for William James at least, partially constructed by feelings of expectancy in the face of fundamental uncertainties.[241]

A willingness to disbelieve, on the other hand, can be similarly informed by self-interest. Aldous Huxley discussed this in *Ends and Means*, where he acknowledged that people sometimes do not find meaning in life because they prefer to avoid the subject altogether:

Most ignorance is invincible ignorance. We don't know because we don't want to know. It is our will that decides how and upon what subjects we shall use our intelligence. Those who detect no meaning in the world generally do so because, for one reason or

---

[240] *Ibid*, p. 11.
[241] *Ibid*, pp. 77-78.

another, it suits their books that the world should be meaningless.[242]

It suited Mortimer J. Adler's books to avoid what he would come to call a "living faith" for much of his life, even though he was a prominent philosophy of religion scholar and professor. Once he did commit himself to the Christian faith with which he had so long been associated, he reflected on his earlier reluctance. He concluded that disbelief lies at the state of one's will, not in the state of one's mind:

> The simple truth of the matter is that I did not wish to live up to being a genuinely religious person. I could not bring myself to will what I ought to will for my whole future if I were to resolve my will, at a particular moment, with regard to religious conversion.[243]

A desire to avoid spirituality in general may have some commonality with a desire to avoid religious commitment. Once a person admits the possibility of the spiritual, and of God, and of the immortality of the soul, scientific materialism loses its monopoly on truth and its articulation of reality. John R. Searle observed, to his obvious chagrin, that the cosmos is either entirely empirically accessible through scientific methodologies, or it is something much larger and more foreboding:

> I believe one of the unstated assumptions behind the current batch of views is that they represent the only scientifically acceptable alternatives to the antiscientism that went along with traditional dualism, the belief in the immortality of the soul, spiritualism, and so

---

[242] Aldous Huxley, *Ends and Means* (New York: Harper & Brothers, 1937): 312.
[243] Mortimer Jerome Adler, *Philosopher at Large: An Intellectual Autobiography* (New York: Macmillan, 1977): 316.

on. Acceptance of the current views is motivated not so much by an independent conviction of their truth as by a terror of what are apparently the only alternatives. That is, the choice we are tacitly left with is between a "scientific" approach, as represented by one or another of the current versions of "materialism," and an "antiscientific" approach, as represented by Cartesianism or some traditional religious conception of the mind.[244]

To use Van Til's terminology, Searle presupposes materialism and naturalism, and this commitment affects and informs his entire scientific project.

Searle's use of the word "terror" in reference to religion and things spiritual is not unique to him. In his book *The Last Word*, Thomas Nagel entitled a chapter "Naturalism and the Fear of Religion." In that chapter he wrote:

> I am talking about...the fear of religion itself. I speak from experience, being strongly subject to this fear myself: I want atheism to be true and am made uneasy by the fact that some of the most intelligent and well-informed people I know are religious believers. It isn't just that I don't believe in God and, naturally, hope that I'm right in my belief. It's that I hope there is no God! I don't want there to be a God; I don't want the universe to be like that.... My guess is that this cosmic authority problem is not a rare condition and that it is responsible for much of the scientism and reductionism

---

[244] John R. Searle, *The Rediscovery of the Mind* (Cambridge, MA: MIT Press, 1992): 3-4.

of our time. One of the tendencies it supports is the ludicrous overuse of evolutionary biology to explain everything about life, including everything about the human mind.[245]

Belief, then, is a choice. Libraries can be filled with books explaining the evidence for and against the possibility of God, immortality and the supernatural, but, to at least some extent, each person chooses whether or not to believe. That choice in turn serves as a presupposition that forms the basis for an entire worldview. People decide to believe or not to believe for their own reasons, and then discover that their entire perspective on life, death, ethics, morality and just about everything else is informed by that worldview.

Recoiling from Disbelief

The Quest for Relief from Purposelessness

Existential dread is not by itself a reason to believe in God or to have faith. It is an experience of imminent, pending loss and a reaction to the possibility or likelihood of the complete annihilation of one's self. The acknowledgment of doom does not necessitate a belief in God, any more than the acknowledgment of one's illness necessitates confidence in any particular health provider or health system.

Even if the case can be made, as in the previous chapter, that faith is the best (if not the only real) solution to the problem of existential dread, this does not compel faith. Again, using the same metaphor, acknowledgment of an illness does not compel confidence in a particular health care provider or health system, even if the track record

---

[245] Thomas Nagel, *The Last Word* (New York: Oxford University Press, 1997): 130-131.

of that provider or system is excellent. A painful or difficult problem provides motivation to consider and weigh options for relief, but such consideration does not always lead everyone to the same choice.

The freedom to will-to-believe, or to will-to-disbelieve, can result in decisions about faith that will vary from person to person irrespective of how compelling the evidence of God and the supernatural might be. This has always been true. An example of this reality is found in Chapter 28 of the Gospel of Matthew, described above.

What existential dread does do, however, is propel us toward a reasonable consideration of possible relief. This motivation has, in turn, informed much of what we have come to recognize as philosophy, psychology and religion. This dynamic has been described in the previous chapters of this work.

The Reluctant Turn to the Vertical

In the book of Ecclesiastes, Qoheleth recoils from the meaninglessness and futility of the horizontal view of life, and in doing so, turns to the vertical, i.e., to God. He makes several observations about God's connection to the existence of humans, the first of which is that God is the creator and is therefore the giver of tasks and activities on this earth.[246] The reader of Ecclesiastes is invited to consider the purpose of life's journey, including the most mundane tasks, not from a horizontal perspective but from the perspective of the Creator-God.[247]

---

[246] Ecclesiastes 7:13-14 ("Consider the work of God: who can make straight what he has made crooked? In the day of prosperity be joyful, and in the day of adversity consider: God has made the one as well as the other, so that man may not find out anything that will be after him.") and 12:7 ("and the dust returns to the earth as it was, and the spirit returns to God who gave it.").

[247] Ecclesiastes 2:24-26 ("There is nothing better for a person than that he should eat and drink and find enjoyment in his toil. This also, I saw, is from the hand of God, for apart from him who can eat or who can have enjoyment? For to the one

From that perspective, human existence may well be an "unhappy business"[248], but it is nevertheless a gift from God that should be well received, well lived, and well appreciated.[249]

But how can the unhappy business of life, with its inevitable trudge toward death, be understood and received as a gift? Qoheleth offers two possible answers to this question. The first answer is directed to non-seekers, that is, to those who, unlike Qoheleth, are not compelled "to seek out and search out by wisdom all that is done under heaven."[250] For these less inquisitorial, less restless, and less esurient folks, Qoheleth recommends a lowering of expectations. To the extent that it is possible to find contentment in life, we should do so.[251] In fact, for most people, the blessings of food, drink, family and productive work, can indeed be sufficient in order to take pleasure in life and to be grateful for life. The unhappy business of life turns out to be much less unhappy once these blessings are recognized and enjoyed wisely and appropriately.

---

who pleases him God has given wisdom and knowledge and joy, but to the sinner he has given the business of gathering and collecting, only to give to one who pleases God. This also is vanity and a striving after wind."); 3:10 ("I have seen the business that God has given to the children of man to be busy with."); 5:18-20 ("Behold, what I have seen to be good and fitting is to eat and drink and find enjoyment[a] in all the toil with which one toils under the sun the few days of his life that God has given him, for this is his lot. Everyone also to whom God has given wealth and possessions and power to enjoy them, and to accept his lot and rejoice in his toil—this is the gift of God. For he will not much remember the days of his life because God keeps him occupied with joy in his heart."); and 8:15 ("And I commend joy, for man has nothing better under the sun but to eat and drink and be joyful, for this will go with him in his toil through the days of his life that God has given him under the sun.").

[248] Ecclesiastes 1:13 ("And I applied my heart to seek and to search out by wisdom all that is done under heaven. It is an unhappy business that God has given to the children of man to be busy with.").

[249] Ecclesiastes 3:13 ("also that everyone should eat and drink and take pleasure in all his toil—this is God's gift to man.").

[250] Ecclesiastes 1:13.

[251] Ecclesiastes 3:13.

But Qoheleth did not write the book of Ecclesiastes primarily for those who are easily contented and amused with life. He wrote it for those who like himself are seekers. Those who are likely to discover that wealth, power, fame, and the pleasures of life have their inherent limits. Once those limits are experienced - either because there is no more opportunity or capacity to increase them, or because it is discovered that they do not satisfy - there is a sense of empty frustration. In a word, vanity.

Once a person discovers that at the end of the day (or, more precisely, at the end of a lifetime), all human effort is, from a horizontal perspective, in vain, it is not inevitable that he or she would turn to the vertical (that is, that they would turn to God). But it is very possible that he or she would do so if, like Qoheleth, they believe that God exists, and that God is the Creator. With these two presuppositions, it is natural and logical for a person who experiences existential emptiness and dread, to turn to God.

This turn to the vertical need not take place solely as the result of an exhaustive search for happiness and meaning. People can choose to look to God as their ultimate source of purpose and meaning, without first seeking fulfillment from a number of other pursuits. But for many people, there is a reluctance to do so, even if they acknowledge God and His role in creation. They seem to have a need to convince themselves of the emptiness of horizontal pursuits, as did Qoheleth, before they resign themselves to find purpose in the vertical.

Not Everyone is Dissatisfied with the Horizontal View

That everything is meaningless under the sun, is both an observation and a pronouncement. Those of Qoheleth's readers who readily understand and empathize with his observations are walked through a thought process with which they are already familiar, joining Qoheleth as he leads them toward God and the duty to fear God and keep his commandments.[252] Ecclesiastes provides for them the assurance that their frustrations with finding significant and enduring meaning in life (that is, their existential dread) is in fact beneficial. It leaves them where they should have been all along: entirely dependent upon God.

Those of Qoheleth's readers who do not naturally grasp and empathize with the gut-wrenching desperation that Qoheleth expresses are also his students. He means to teach this latter group by mapping out for them a series of stories and proverbs that shine a light on life's inevitable futility. He invites these students to join him on his journey from futility to faith. He attempts to shake for them the foundations of their lives, so that they gratefully look to and receive a kingdom that cannot be shaken.[253] However, if they choose not to join him on that journey, he wishes them well. Enjoy life under the sun, he suggests, if that's all there is in your understanding. Without God, life is too short to be anxious about wealth, power, fame, pleasure and the like. Be satisfied with what you have, especially if dissatisfaction does not carry you vertically to God.

The Gift of Dread

The dynamic pattern of futility leading to faith is not unique to Ecclesiastes. While this dynamic seems to be exaggerated in the life of Solomon, it is experienced less dramatically all of the time. Testimonies of those who have come to faith in Jesus Christ, for example, are often peppered with stories about how various human pursuits, from education to promiscuity, to drugs and alcoho,l to fame and fortune, etc., ultimately proved to be disappointing, unsatisfying and pointless. It is only after these horizontal pursuits run their course, or result in

---

[252] Ecclesiastes 12:13-14.
[253] *See* Hebrews 12:28.

grave consequences, that many people arrive at an epiphany of faith. In the telling of these stories, furthermore, is often acknowledged that had it not been for the experiencing of the limitations of such pursuits, all of the benefits of the turn to the vertical would not have been realized. Expressions such as, "had I not crashed and burned," or, "had I not hit the wall," are often accompanied by expressions of gratitude for having experienced the desperation of such consequences.

In other words, the limits of horizontal human endeavors force us to look upwards. This dynamic is common to the human experience. It involves what G.K. Chesterton called "the game of self-limitation."[254] Our inherent "longing for larger and larger horizons"[255] forces us to react to, and work within, limits in order to achieve greater things than would have been achieved had there been no such limits:

> The imagination is supposed to work towards the infinite; though in that sense the infinite is the opposite of the imagination. For the imagination deals with an image. And an image is in its nature a thing that has an outline and therefore a limit.[256]

Once limits are discovered, the near-universal human response is to draw on imagination, creativity, reasoning skills, and every other human capacity, to overcome or flourish within, that limit. This, Chesterton observes, is the essence of some of our favorite stories, such as Robinson Crusoe:

---

[254] G.K. Chesterton and Randall Paine, *The Autobiography of G.K. Chesterton* (San Francisco, CA: Ignatius Press, 2006), p. 112.
[255] *Ibid*, p. 111. This longing is alluded to in Ecclesiastes 3:11: "He has made everything beautiful in its time. Also, he has put eternity into man's heart, yet so that he cannot find out what God has done from the beginning to the end."
[256] *Ibid.*

The charm of Robinson Crusoe is not in the fact that
he could find his way to a remote island; but in the fact
that he could not find any way of getting away from
it. It is that fact which gives an intensive interest and
excitement to all the things that he had with him on
the island; the acts and the parrot and the guns and the
little horde of grain.[257]

The case has been made in Chapter Two of this work that the
human experience is characterized by a search for meaning and
purpose. At Chapter Three, the psychological need to find purpose
and meaning was observed and explored. Chapters Four and Five have
given consideration to the theological notion that people have "eternity
in their hearts" and that the subsequent yearning for the supernatural
and the eternal prompts us to seek God.

Despite this built-in sense of emptiness and restlessness that leads
to a sense of dread, not everyone chooses to seek God. As seen above,
the acknowledgment of God and the eternal is a choice made by
each person. A preference to serve the interests of self rather than the
interests of God can nudge a person in the direction of a rejection of
God. So can a preference for autonomy and the avoidance of moral
accountability. A commitment to naturalism, as expressed by John
Searle, may be appealing because all of reality is accessible through
science and there is no need to be concerned about all of the possibilities
that the supernatural might represent. In short, it is not difficult to
understand why God and the supernatural would be rejected ... so
long as it is understood that there is plenty of evidence and abundant
arguments that make the opposite choice reasonable and rational.

The difficulty experienced by many of those who reject God and
the supernatural, however, is that they are left with dread. That is, they

---

[257] *Ibid*, pp. 111-112.

are unable to arrive at a robust sense of purpose and meaning in life. Like Augustine, Adler, and millions of others throughout history, they experience a certain restlessness. A discomfort that is philosophically, psychologically and spiritually disquieting. An existential angst. In a word, dread.

To the extent that such dread drives them back to God (as it did for Augustine and Adler and millions of others throughout history), it is a gift. It is grace. It is a mechanism by which the futility of life without God can be considered and, following the pattern of Qoheleth, a proper acknowledgment of who God is can accompany a proper acknowledgment of who we are as human beings created by God.

REFERENCES

Addad, Moshe. "Psychogenic Neuroticism and Noogenic Self-Strengthening." *International Forum for Logotherapy* 10 (1987): 52-59.

Adherents.com, "Major Religions of the World Ranked by Number of Adherents," http://adherents.com/Relitions_by_Adherents.html (accessed at February 3, 2012).

Adler, Mortimer Jerome. *Philosopher at Large: An Intellectual Autobiography.* New York: Macmillan, 1977.

Allen, Prudence. "Person and Complementarity in *Fides et eatio*," in Foster, David Ruel, and Joseph W. Koterski. *The Two Wings of Catholic Thought: Essays on Fides et ratio.* Washington, D.C.: Catholic University of America Press, 2003.

American Psychiatric Association. *Diagnostic and Statistical Manual of Mental Disorders DSM-IV-TR.* Arlington, VA: American Psychiatric Assoc, 2010.

Avramenko, Richard. "The Wound and Salve of Time: Augustine's Politics of Human Happiness." *The Review of Metaphysics* no. 60 (June 2007): 779-811.

Archer, Margaret S. "Resisting the Revival of Relativism" *International Sociology*, 2, no. 3 (Sept., 1987), pp. 235-250.

Asa, Robert. "The Faith of a Skeptic: The Enigma of Ecclesiastes." *Journal for the Liberal Arts and Sciences* 13, no. 3 (2009): 55-66.

Augustine, Saint. *Confessions*, translated by Edward Bouverie Pusey. New York: Book of the Month Club, 1996. Also available from http://www.classicreader.com/book/1738/1/. Accessed 29 July 2013.

Barkley, Russell A. *Taking Charge of Adult ADHD*. New York: Guilford Press, 2010.

Barnes, Robert C. "Viktor Frankl's Logotherapy: Spirituality and Meaning in the New Millennium," *Texas Counseling Association Journal*. 28, no. 1 (Spring 2000): 24-31.

Barrett, David B., George T. Kurian & Todd M. Mohnson, *World Christian Encyclopedia, vol. 1*. New York: Oxford University Press, 2001.

Bannink, Fredrike P. "Posttraumatic Success: Solution-Focused Brief Therapy". *Brief Treatment and Crisis Intervention*. 8, no. 3 (2008): 215-225.

Baumeister, Roy F. *Meanings of Life*. New York: Guilford Press, 1991.

Benatar, David. *Life, Death & Meaning: Key Philosophical Readings on the Big Questions.* Lanham, Md: Rowman & Littlefield Publishers, 2004.

Bentham, Jeremy. "Cooperation: Intended Speech, 1825" in John Stuart Mill and John M. Robson. *Journals and Debating Speeches* (Toronto: University of Toronto Press, 1988).

Bergler, Edmund. "On the Disease-Entity Boredom ('Alysosis') and its Psychopathology," *Psychiatric Quarterly* 19, no. 1 (January 1945): 38-51.

Billy Graham Evangelistic Association, "Steps to Peace with God," available from http://www.billygraham.org/SH StepsToPeace. asp. Accessed 29 July 2013.

Booker, Mike, and Mark Ireland. *Evangelism – Which Way Now?: An Evaluation of Alpha, Emmaus, Cell Church and Other Contemporary Strategies for Evangelism.* London: Church House, 2003.

Brown, Lily A., Brandon A. Gaudiano, and Ivan W. Miller. "Investigating the Similarities and Differences between Practitioners of Second- and Third-Wave Cognitive-Behavioral Therapies". *Behavior Modification* 35, no. 2 (2011): 187-200.

Bulka Reuven P. "Logotherapy and Talmudic Judaism," *Journal of Religion and Health* 14, no. 4 (1975): 277.

Burns, Elizabeth. "What Happens After Pascal's Wager: Living Faith and Rational Belief - Daniel Garber," *The Philosophical Quarterly* 61, no. 242 (2011): 218-221.

Camus, Albert. *The Myth of Sisyphus and Other Essays*. Translated by Justin O'Brien. New York: Vintage Books, 1955.

Campus Crusade for Christ International "Four Spiritual Laws," available from ERLINK"http://www.campuscrusade.com/fourlawseng.htm."http://www.campuscrusade.com/fourlawseng.htm. Accessed 29 July 2013.

Catholic Church, and John Paul. *Encyclical Letter, Fides Et Ratio, of the Supreme Pontiff John Paul II: To the Bishops of the Catholic Church on the Relationship between Faith and Reason*. Washington, D.C.: United States Catholic Conference, 1998.

Chesterton, G.K. and Randall Paine. *The Autobiography of G.K. Chesterton*. San Francisco: Ignatius, 2006.

Chulef, Ada S., Stephen J. Read and David A. Walsh, "A Hierarchical Taxonomy of Human Goals," *Motivation and Emotion* 25, no. 3 (September 2001): 191-232.

Cherry, Conrad, *The Theology of Jonathan Edwards: A Reappraisal*. New York: Doubleday and Company, Inc., 1966.

Crandall, James E. and Roger D. Rasmussen, *Journal of Clinical Psychology* 31 (1975):483-485

Cross, F. L. *The Oxford Dictionary of the Christian Church*. London: Oxford University Press, 1966..

Crumbaugh, James C. "Frankl's Logotherapy: A New Orientation in Meaning." *Journal of Religion and Health*. 10 no. 4 (October 1971): 373-386.

Crumbaugh, James C., and Leonard T. Maholick. "An Experimental Study in Existentialism: The Psychometric Approach to Frankl's Concept of Noogenic Neurosis" *Journal of Clinical Psychology* (1964): 589-596.

— *Manual of Instructions for the Purpose-in- Life Test.* Munster, Ind.: Psychometric Affiliates, 1969.

Damon, William, Jenni Menon, and Kendall Cotton Bronk. "The Development of Purpose During Adolescence." *Applied Developmental Science 7*, no. 3 (July 2003): 119-128.

Debats, Louis Dominique, Petra M. Van der Lubbe and Fimmy R.A. Wezeman, "On the Psychometric Properties of the Life Regard Index (LRI): A Measure of Meaningful Life," *Personality and Individual Differences* 14, no. 2 (February 1993): 337-345.

de Unamuno, Miguel. *The Tragic Sense of Life in Men and Nations.* Trans. Anthony Kerrigan. Ed. Anthony Kerrigan and Martin Nozick. Bollingen Series 85, no. 4. Princeton, N.J.: Princeton University Press, 1972.

Dickinson, Emily. *The Complete Poems of Emily Dickinson.* Boston: Back Bay Books, 1960.

Diogenes, Allen, and Eric O. Springsted. *Philosophy for Understanding Theology.* Louisville: Westminster John Knox Press, 2007.

Edmunds, Lowell. *Approaches to Greek Myth.* Baltimore: Johns Hopkins University Press, 1990.

Edwards, Jonathan. *Religious Affections*, volume 2 of *The Works of Jonathan Edwards*, edited John E. Smith. New Haven: Yale University Press, 1959. Also available from http://www.leaderu. com/cyber/books/religaffect/rapt1sec1.html Accessed 29 July 2013.

— *Treatise on Grace*, edited by Paul Helm. Cambridge: James Clark, 1971.

— *Images or Shadows of Divine Things*, in *Typological Writings*, vol. 11 of *The Works of Jonathan Edwards*, ed. by Wallace E. Anderson. New Haven: Yale University Press, 1948.

Ellenberger, Henri F. "A Clinical Introduction to Psychiatric Phenomenology and Existential Analysis." In May, Rollo, and Ludwig Binswanger. *Existence; a New Dimension in Psychiatry and Psychology* (New York: Basic Books, 1958): 92-124.

Ellis, Albert. *Reason and Emotion in Psychotherapy*. Secaucus, N.J.: Citadel Press, 1962.

Evans, C. Stephen. *Faith Beyond Reason: A Kierkegaardian Account.* Grand Rapids, Mich: W.B. Eerdmans Pub, 1998.

Fabry, Dagmar Devorah Sigrid, Alia Sheikh and Matthew Selman, "Logotherapy can Enrich Cognitive Behavioral Therapy Practice," *The International Forum for Logotherapy* 30 (2007): 100-106.

Fabry, Joseph. "The Calls of Meaning," in *The Human Quest for Meaning: A Handbook of Psychological Research and Clinical Applications*, edited by Wong, Paul T. P., and Prem S. Fry, 295-305. Mahwah, N.J.: Lawrence Erlbaum Associates, 1998.

Farmer, Richard, and Norman Sundberg. "Boredom Proneness – The Development and Correlates of a New Scale." *Journal of Personality Assessment*. 50, no. 1 (1986): 4-17.

Farnsworth, Kirk E. "Despair that Restores" *Psychotherapy: Theory, Research & Practice* 12, no. 1 (Spring 1975): 44-47.

Finney, John. *Finding Faith Today: How Does It Happen?* Swindon: British and Foreign Bible Society, 1999.

Frankl, Viktor E. *Man's Search for Meaning: An Introduction to Logotherapy*. Boston: Beacon Press, 1992.

— *Man's Search for Ultimate Meaning*. New York: Insight Books, 1997.

— *The Doctor and the Soul: From Psychotherapy to Logotherapy*. New York: Vintage Books, 1986.

— "The Philosophical Foundations of Logotherapy." In Erwin W. Straus, *Phenomenology: Pure and Applied; The First Lexington Conference*. Pittsburgh: Duquesne University Press, 1964.

— *The Will to Meaning: Foundations and Applications of Logotherapy*. New York: Meridian, 1988.

Freeman, Kathleen, and Hermann Diels. *Ancilla to The Pre-Socratic Philosophers: A Complete Translation of the Fragments in Diels Fragmente Der Vorsokratiker*. Oxford: Basil Blackwell, 1956.

Friedman, Thomas L. *The World Is Flat: A Brief History of the Twenty-First Century*. New York: Farrar, Straus and Giroux, 2006.

Garber Daniel. *What Happens After Pascal's Wager: Living Faith and Rational Belief.* Milwaukee, WI: Marquette University Press, 2009.

Ganzevoort, R. Ruard. "Theory and Practice - Religious Coping Reconsidered, Part One: An Integrated Approach." *Journal of Psychology and Theology* 26, no. 3 (1998): 260-275.

— "Theory and Practice - Religious Coping Reconsidered, Part Two: A Narrative Reformulation". *Journal of Psychology and Theology* 26, no. 3 (1998): 276-286.

Gault, Brian P. "A Reexamination of 'Eternity' in Ecclesiastes 3:11, *Biblotheca Sacra* 165 (January-March 2008): 39-57.

Geisler, Norman L., and David Geisler. *Conversational Evangelism.* Eugene, Or: Harvest House Publishers, 2009.

Geisler, Norman L., and Frank Turek. *I Don't Have Enough Faith to Be an Atheist.* Wheaton, Ill: Crossway Books, 2004.

Ginsburg, Christian David. *The Song of Songs and Coheleth (Commonly Called the Book of Ecclesiastes) ; Translated from the Original Hebrew, with a Commentary, Historical and Critical.* New York: KTVA Publ. House, 1970.

Gruner, LeRoy. "Heroin, Hashish, and Hallelujah: The Search for Meaning." *Review of Religious Research.* 26, no. 2 (1984): 176-186.

Habermas, Gary R., and Mike Licona. *The Case for the Resurrection of Jesus.* Grand Rapids, MI: Kregel Publications, 2004.

Harlow, Lisa L., Michael D. Newcomb, and P.M. Bentler, "Depression, Self-derogation, Substance Use, and Suicide Ideation: Lack of Purpose in Life as a Mediational Factor," *Journal of Clinical Psychology* 42, no. 1 (January 1986): 5-21.

Hawking, Stephen W. and Leonard Mlodinow. *The Grand Design.* New York: Bantam Books, 2010.

Healy, Seán Desmond. *Boredom, Self, and Culture.* Rutherford: Fairleigh Dickinson University Press, 1984.

Heidegger, Martin. *Being and Time.* Translated by John Macquarrie and Edward Robinson. New York: Harper and Row, 1962.

— "What is Metaphysics? in *Existence and Being,* edited by W. Brock. Chicago: Henry Regnery Co., 1949.

Heschel, Abraham Joshua. *Who Is Man?* Stanford, Calif: Stanford University Press, 1965.

Holmes, Mark. "A Response to Bowers, Howard, Stanley and Soltis," *American Journal of Education,* 94, no. 4 (Aug., 1986), pp. 537-541.

Hulse Erroll. *The Great Invitation: Examining the Use of the Invitation System in Evangelism.* Welwyn: Evangelical, 1986.

Hutzell, Robert R. "A Review of the Purpose in Life Test," *The International Forum for Logotherapy* 11 (1988): 89–101.

Huxley, Aldous. *Ends and Means.* New York: Harper & Brothers, 1937.

International Council for Catechesis, "Adult Catechesis and the Christian Community: Some Principles and Guidelines" (Libreria

Editrice Vaticana/St. Paul Publications, 1990). Available from http://www.vatican.va/roman_curia/congregations/cclergy/documents/rc_con_cclergy_doc_14041990_acat_en.html. Accessed 29 July 2013.

IslamReligion.com, at http://www.islamreligion.com/articles/204/, Accessed 29 July 2013.

James, William. *The Will to Believe: And Other Essays in Popular Philosophy, Human Immortality; Two Supposed Objections to the Doctrine.* New York: Dover, 1956.

Kant, Immanuel. *Critique of Practical Reason.* New York: Liberal Arts Press, 1956.

Kendall, Elizabeth. "Psychosocial Adjustment Following Closed Head Injury: A Model for Understanding Individual Differences and Predicting Outcome." *Neuropsychological Rehabilitation: An International Journal* 6, no. 2 (1996): 101-132.

Kernan, Julie. *Our Friend, Jacques Maritain: A Personal Memoir.* Garden City, N.Y.: Doubleday, 1975.

Kernberg, Otto F. "A psychoanalytic model for the classification of personality disorders." In M. Achenheil, B. Bondy, R. Engel, M. Ermann, & N. Nedopil (Eds.), *Implications of Psychopharmacology to Psychiatry: Biological, Nosological, and Therapeutical Concepts.* New York: Springer, 1996: 66-78.

Kierkegaard Søren. *Fear and Trembling.* Edited by C. Stephen Evans, and Sylvia Walsh. Cambridge: Cambridge University Press, 2006.

—*The Practice of Christianity*, translated by Howard V. Hong and Edna H. Hong. Princeton: Princeton University Press, 1991.

—*The Sickness unto Death: A Christian Psychological Exposition for Upbuilding and Awakening*. Edited and translated by Howard V. Hong, and Edna H. Hong. Princeton, N.J.: Princeton University Press, 1980.

Kierkegaard, Søren and Alastair Hannay. *Either/or: A Fragment of Life*. London, England: Penguin Books, 1992.

— *The Sickness Unto Death: A Christian Psychological Exposition for Edification and Awakening*. London, England: Penguin Books, 1989.

Kierkegaard, Søren, Howard V. Hong, and Edna H. Hong. *The Sickness unto Death: A Christian Psychological Exposition for Upbuilding and Awakening*. Princeton, N.J.: Princeton University Press, 1980.

— *Fear and Trembling; Repetition*. Princeton, N.J.: Princeton University Press, 1983.

— *The Point of View*. Princeton, N.J.: Princeton University Press, 1998.

— *Concluding Unscientific Postscript to Philosophical Fragments*. Princeton, N.J.: Princeton University Press, 1992.

Klinger, Eric. "The Search for Meaning in Evolutionary Perspective and Its Clinical Implications," in *The Human Quest for Meaning: A Handbook of Psychological Research and Clinical Applications* edited by Wong, Paul T. P. and Prem S. Fry. Mahwah, N.J.: Lawrence Erlbaum Associates, 1998.

Lantz, Jim and Jan Lantz, "Franklian Psychotherapy with Adults Molested as Children," *Journal of Religion and Health* 42, no. 4 (Winter 1992): 297-307.

Laslett, Peter. *Philosophy, Politics and Society; A Collection.* Oxford: Blackwell, 1956.

Lester, David and Souhel Badro, "Depression, Suicidal Preoccupation and Purpose in Life in a Subclinical Population," *Personality and Individual Differences* 13, no. 1 (1992): 75-76.

Lewis, C. S. *Mere Christianity: A Revised and Amplified Edition, with a New Introduction, of the Three Books, Broadcast Talks, Christian Behaviour, and Beyond Personality.* San Francisco: HarperSanFrancisco, 2001.

Lindbeck, George. "Forward" In *By the Renewing of Your Minds: The Pastoral Function of Christian Doctrine,* edited by Ellen T. Charry, xiii-xiv. New York: Oxford University Press, 1997.

Longman, Tremper, III. *The Book of Ecclesiastes.* Grand Rapids: Eerdmans, 1998.

Lyotard, Jean-François. *The Postmodern Condition: A Report on Knowledge.* Minneapolis: University of Minnesota Press, 1984.

Maddi, Salvatore R., Marnie Brwo, Doborah M. Khoshaba, and Mark Vaitkus, "Relationship of Hardiness and Religiousness to Depression and Anger," *Consulting Psychology Journal* 58, no. 3 (Summer 2006): 148-161.

Mahoney, Michael J. "Introduction to Special Section: Theoretical Developments in Cognitive Psychotherapies," *Journal of Consulting and Clinical Psychology* 61, no. 2 (1993): 187-193.

Marcel, Gabriel. *The Philosophy of Existentialism*. New York: Citadel Press, 2002.

Martin, Richard P. *Myths of the Ancient Greeks*. New York: New American Library, 2003.

Maslow, Abraham. "A theory of human motivation." *Psychological Review* 50 (1943): 370-396.

May, Henry F.. *The Enlightenment In America*. London: Oxford University Press, 1976.

May, Rollo. *Existential Psychology, Second Edition*. New York: Random House, 1961.

Mayers, Ronald B. *Balanced Apologetics: Using Evidences and Presuppositions in Defense of the Faith*. Grand Rapids, MI: Kregel Publications, 1996.

McIntyre, Patrick. *The Graham Formula*. Mammoth Spring, AR: White Harvest Publishing, 2005.

Melton, Amanda M.A. and Stefan E. Schulenberg. "On the Measurement of Meaning: Logotherapy's Empirical Contributions to Humanistic Psychology." *The Humanistic Psychologist*, 36 (2008): 31-44.

— "On the Relationship between Meaning in Life and Boredom Proneness: Examining a Logotherapy Postulate." *Psychological Reports* 101, no. 3F (December 2007): 1016-1022.

Mill, John Stuart and John M. Robson. *Journals and Debating Speeches.* Toronto: University of Toronto Press, 1988.

Miller, Donald E. *Reinventing American Protestantism: Christianity in the New Millennium.* Berkely, CA: University of California Press, 1997.

Mishali, Moshe, Ronit Endevelt, and Anthony D. Heymann. "The 'Emphatic Narrative': A New Tool for Obesity Treatment". *Nutrition Today.* 46, no. 1 (2010): 27-32.

Monton, Bradley, "Mixed Strategies Can't Evade Pascal's Wager." *Analysis* 71, no. 4 (2011): 642-645.

Mumford, Lewis. *The Pentagon of Power.* New York: Harcourt Brace Jovanovich, 1970.

Nagel, Thomas. *The Last Word.* New York: Oxford University Press, 1997.

Nietzsche, Friedrich. *The Gay Science,* edited by Bernard Williams, translated by Josefine Nauckhoff and Adrian Del Caro. New York: Cambridge University Press, 2001.

Nietzsche, Friedrich Wilhem and Walter Arnold Kaufmann. *The Gay Science; With a Prelude in Rhymes and an Appendix of Songs.* New York: Vintage Books, 1974.

Pargament, Kenneth I., Harold G. Koenig, and Lisa M. Perez. "The Many Methods of Religious Coping: Development and Initial Validation of the RCOPE," *Journal of Clinical Psychology* 56, no. 4 (2000): 519-43.

Park, Crystal. "Religiousness/Spirituality and Health: A Meaning Systems Perspective." *Journal of Behavioral Medicine* 30, no. 4 (2007): 319-328.

Pascal, Blaise. *Pensées*, translated by Roger Ariew. Indianapolis, IN: Hackett Publishing Co., 2005.

— *Pensées*, translated by A.J. Kraisheimer. London: Penguin Books, 1995.

— *Pensées*, translated by W.F. Trotter. Mineola, NY: Dover Publications, 2003.

Petsche, Johanna. "Religion, God and the Meaninglessness of it all in Woody Allen's Thought and Films," *Sydney Studies in Religion*, 2009. http://escholarship.usyd.edu.au/journals/index.php/SSR/article/view/712 (accessed at January 27, 2012).

Patrick McIntyre, *The Graham Formula: Why most Decisions for Christ are Ineffective.* Mammoth Springs, AR: White Harvest, 2005.

Plantinga, Alvin. *Warranted Christian Belief.* New York: Oxford University Press, 2000.

Plato, "Apology of Socrates," in Thomas G. West and Grace Starry West, trans., *Four Texts on Socrates: Plato's Euthyphro, Apology, and Crito and Aristophanes' Clouds*. Ithaca, NY: Cornell University Press, 1984.

— *Plato's Phaedo: Literally Translated*. Trans. Edward Meredith Cope. Cambridge: University Press, 1875.

— *Protagoras and Meno*. Penguin Classics. London: Penguin Books, 2005.

Plato, and Donald J. Zeyl. *Gorgias*. Indianapolis: Hackett Pub. Co, 1987.

Power, Michael J., and Chris Brewin, *The Transformation of Meaning in Psychological Therapies: Integrating Theory and Practice*. Chichester, England: Wiley, 1997.

Rasmussen, Douglas B., and Douglas J. Den Uyl. *Liberty and Nature: An Aristotelian Defense of Liberal Order*. La Salle, Ill: Open Court, 1991.

Robak, Rostyslaw W. and Paul W. Griffin, "Purpose in Life: What is its Relationship to Happiness, Depression, and Grieving?" *North American Journal of Psychology* 2, no. 1 (2000): 113-119.

Rorty, Richard. *Philosophy and the Mirror of Nature*. Princeton: Princeton University Press, 1979.

Sartre, Jean-Paul. "Existentialism is a Humanism," in Walter Kaufman, editor. *Existentialism from Dostoevsky to Sartre*. New York: World Publishing, 1965.

— *Being and Nothingness; An Essay on Phenomenological Ontology.* New York: Philosophical Library, 1956.1965.

— *Nausea,* trans. Lloyd Alexander. New York: New Directions, 1964.

Sartre, Jean-Paul, and George Joseph Becker. *Anti-Semite and Jew.* New York: Schocken Books, 1965.

Schaeffer, Francis A. *The Church at the End of the Twentieth Century ; Including, The Church Before the Watching World.* Wheaton, Ill: Crossway Books, 1994.

Schopenhauer, Arthur, and Eric Francis Jules Payne. [*Die Welt Als Wille Und Vorstellung.*] *The World As Will and Representation, Volume II,* Translated by E.F.J. Payne. New York: Dover, 1966.

Schulenberg, Stefan E., Robert R. Hutzell, Carrie Nassif and Julius M. Rogina. "Logotherapy for Clinical Practice." *Psychotherapy: Theory, Research, Practice, Training,* 45, no. 4 (2008): 447-463.

Schulenberg, Stefan E., Lindsay W. Schnetzer, Michael R. Winters and Robert R. Hutzell, "Meaning-Centered Couples Therapy: Logotherapy and Intimate Relationships," *Journal of Contemporary Psychotherapy* 40 (2010): 95-102.

Scobie, Geoffrey E. W. *Psychology of Religion.* New York: Wiley, 1975.

Searle, John R. *The Rediscovery of the Mind.* Cambridge, MA: MIT Press, 1992.

Shakespeare, William. *The Complete Works of William Shakespeare* (New York: World Syndicate, 1970).

Shek, Daniel T.L. "Measurement in Pessimism in Chinese Adolescents: The Chinese Hopelessness Scale," *Social Behavior and Personality,* 21, no. 2 (1993): 107-119.

— "Meaning in Life and Adjustment in Midlife Parents in Hong Kong," *International Forum for Logotherapy* 17, no. 2 (1994): 102-107.

Sire, James W. *Why Should Anyone Believe Anything at All?* Downers Grove, Ill: InterVarsity Press, 1994.

Smidt, Kobus de. "The Human Freedom fo Find Meaning: A Logo-Philosophical Reading of Revelation 1:3," *Missionalia* 33, no. 3 (November 2005): 510-531.

Smith, Steven D. The *Disenchantment of Secular Discourse.* Cambridge, Mass: Harvard University Press, 2010.

Soderstrom, Henrik, Maria Rastam and Christopher Gillberg, "Temperament and Character in Adults with Asperger Syndrome," *Autism* 6, no.3 (2002) 287-297.

Solomon, Robert C. *The Passions: Emotions and the Meaning of Life.* Indianapolis: Hackett Pub. Co, 1993.

— *Dark Feelings, Grim Thoughts: Experience and Reflection in Camus and Sartre.* Oxford: Oxford University Press, 2006.

Stace, Walter T., "Man Against Darkness," in *The Meaning of Life: Questions, Answers, and Analysis,* edited by Steven Sanders and David R. Cheney. Englewood Cliffs, N.J.: Prentice-Hall, 1980.

Stark, Rodney. "Secularization, R.I.P." *Sociology of Religion* 60, no. 3 (October 1, 1999): 249-273.

Stark, Rodney and Roger Finke. *Acts of Faith: Explaining the Human Side of Religion.* Berkely: University of Califorinia Press, 2000.

Stein, Edward. *Without Good Reason: The Rationality Debate in Philosophy and Cognitive Science.* Oxford: Clarendon Press, 1996.

TheBuddhaGarden.com, at http://TheBuddhaGarden.com/convert-to-buddhism.htm, Accessed 29 July 2013.

Tillich, Paul. *The Courage to Be.* New Haven: Yale University Press, 1952.

Tix, Andrew P. and Patricia F. Frazier. "The Use of Religious Coping During Stressful Life Events: Main Effects, Moderation, and Mediation." *Journal of Consulting and Clinical Psychology.* 66, no. 2 (1998): 411-422.

Trevino, Kelly M., Kenneth I. Pargament, Sian Cotton, Anthony C. Leonard, June Hahn, Caron Ann Caprini-Faigin, and Joel Tsevat, ""Religious Coping and Physiological, Psychological, Social, and Spiritual Outcomes in Patients with HIV/AIDS: Cross-Sectional and Longitudinal Findings," *AIDS and Behavior.* 14, no. 2 (2010): 379-389..

Turner, James. *Without God, Without Creed.* Baltimore: The John Hopkins University Press, 1985.

Tyrer, Peter, Mitchard, Sarah, Methuen, Caroline and Ranger, Maja. "Treatment Rejecting and Treatment Seeking Personality

Disorders: Type R and Type S." *Journal of Personality Disorders* *17*, no. 3 (2003): 263-268.

Weber, Max, Peter Baehr, and Gordon C. Wells. *The Protestant Ethic and the "Spirit" of Capitalism and Other Writings*. New York: Penguin Books, 2002.

Weinstein, Lawrence, Xiaolin Xie, and Charalambos C. Cleanthous. "Purpose in Life, Boredom and Volunteerism in a Group of Retirees," *Psychological Reports* 76, no. 2 (April 1995): 482.

West, Thomas G. and Grace Starry West. *Four texts on Socrates: Plato's Euthyphro, Apology and Crito and Aristophanes' Clouds*. Ithaca, NY: Cornell University Press, 1998.

Wong, Paul T.P. "Meaning Therapy: An Integrative and Positive Existential Psychotherapy". *Journal of Contemporary Psychotherapy*. 40, no. 2 (2010): 85-93.

Whybray, Roger Norman. *Ecclesiastes*. Grand Rapids: Eerdmans, 1989.

Williams, Clifford. *Existential Reasons for Belief in God: A Defense of Desires and Emotions for Faith*. Downers Grove, IL: IVP Academic, 2011.

Yalom, Irvin D.. *Existential Psychotherapy*. New York: Basic Books, 1980.

www.ingramcontent.com/pod-product-compliance
Lightning Source LLC
Chambersburg PA
CBHW071439090426
42737CB00011B/1712